500

THE REBEL ENTREPRENEUR

THE REBEL ENTREPRENEUR

REWRITING THE BUSINESS RULEBOOK

JONATHAN MOULES

KoganPage

LONDON · PHILADELPHIA · NEW DELHI

First published in Great Britain and the United States in 2012 by Kogan Page Limited

120 Pentonville Road	1518 Walnut Street, Suite 1100	4737/23 Ansari Road
London N1 9JN	Philadelphia PA 19102	Daryaganj
United Kingdom	USA	New Delhi 110002
www.koganpage.com		India

© Jonathan Moules, 2012

The right of Jonathan Moules to be identified as the author of this work has been asserted by him in accordance with the Copyright, Designs and Patents Act 1988.

ISBN   978 0 7494 6482 0
E-ISBN   978 0 7494 6483 7

British Library Cataloguing-in-Publication Data

A CIP record for this book is available from the British Library.

Library of Congress Cataloging-in-Publication Data

Moules, Jonathan.
  The rebel entrepreneur : rewriting the business rulebook / Jonathan Moules. – 1st ed.
    p. cm.
  Includes index.
    ISBN 978-0-7494-6482-0 – ISBN 978-0-7494-6483-7   1. Entrepreneurship.   2. Success in business.   I. Title.
  HB615.M688 2012
  658.4′21–dc23
                                                      2012010357

Typeset by Graphicraft Limited, Hong Kong
Print production managed by Jellyfish
Printed and bound by CPI Group (UK) Ltd, Croydon, CR0 4YY

Contents

Prologue: The importance of being a rebel

Success in business is a minority sport.

In most developed countries, the overwhelming majority of all privately held enterprises are small – about 95 per cent, according to the OECD. The vast majority of these are sole traders. There is also an incredibly high failure rate among new ventures. About 8 out of every 10 of the companies started each year do not make it to their fifth birthday. Only a small percentage of those businesses that manage to struggle on beyond infancy then go on to create the real growth drivers of an economy.

However, it is these companies that are so important to the success of economies, providing new products and services that raise standards of living and, perhaps most importantly, the vast majority of new jobs. Just 7 per cent of businesses are responsible for more than half of all the new employment created in the UK economy, according to the British think tank Nesta. This figure is about the same across developed nations, according to the OECD, the economic body that measures such things. Nesta went further in its analysis, noting that these job-creating growth businesses are also very young as organizations.

This is a very exclusive club of companies indeed. What is it that makes these companies different? One way to define them and their leadership is as rule breakers. I am not saying that these companies have to be involved in illegal behaviour. No. It is that they are often created and run by people who see that you get ahead by going against the received wisdom on how to grow a business.

Call them rebel entrepreneurs, if you like. That is what this book is about.

What I hope to show you is the way that such entrepreneurs have defied the conventional views about how someone should behave in order to make their business more successful, even world beating. To do this, I have picked eight areas where a company can make a difference. They relate to finance, pricing, leadership, business models, cost management, sales strategies, the need to change and fear of failure.

Throughout the chapters I will introduce you to companies that I think exemplify the characteristics of rebel entrepreneurs in the way they have challenged conventional wisdom. Among them are companies that have been around for centuries, like knitwear producer John Smedley, which can date its origins back to the time of the American War of Independence. Alongside companies like this I look at some of the ways the young stars of the internet age, like Twitter, have been able to succeed.

I have also sought to include some of the best academic research on the subject of start-ups to show how the truth about entrepreneurship and business ownership is not what people always think.

The topics I have chosen for this book reflect the breadth of issues an entrepreneur has to consider when building a company. Each is a journey through tips I have picked up during six years of writing about entrepreneurship for the *Financial Times*.

There are many more subjects I could have covered because entrepreneurship is a many-faceted discipline. This is a good thing for me because it means that, if this book proves interesting to a lot of people, I have plenty of scope for a second volume.

Indeed, the idea of selling more of what you already have to the people who already like it rather than wasting time, energy and money on capturing new markets is one of the lessons of this book, so I can also show that I can practise what I preach.

Hopefully you will find a lot more useful advice in this book either to help you build a better company or perhaps inspire you to have a go at chasing that idea you have nurtured for an enterprise.

As I have discovered with this book, the journey to success can be a long one, but then those are usually the ones worth taking.

I hope you enjoy this book.

Chapter One
Funding is
for fools

I must start by saying that this is probably the most difficult chapter of this book to write. Money and people are the sources of some of the biggest challenges, and most passionate disagreements, that founders and business owners face. This is because these two key elements of any enterprise strike at the heart of what a business is all about: generating profit from the actions of human beings. As a result, they are also subject to some of the most firmly ingrained assumptions about business, which are not always right for a business to succeed.

The point of this book is to take some alternative opinions on some of the main areas of concern in a business. The idea is to show that acting in a way that does not follow the crowd can be a better way of managing your business if you really want to grow bigger and faster – what I call being a rebel entrepreneur.

We will return to people issues in the later chapters. But first, let's tackle money. There are several clichés about money. Some are true, however, such as cash is king. A company can survive without profits and even, for a period, without any sales, but if there is no cash in the coffers to pay the bills the venture is insolvent and therefore cannot trade legally.

Money, or rather the lack of it, has been front page news around the world for several years, first with the credit squeeze, then, following the collapse of Lehman Brothers in September 2008, the danger of a full-blown banking collapse. The narrative for most business owners is that the banks have turned off the taps of finance and are therefore destroying enterprise. This, unlike the cash is king cliché, is only half true. The inconvenient truth is that some businesses should never have been given the money in the first place.

One of the little discussed tragedies of the financial mismanagement of the noughties was the way the actions of the banking sector gave the impression to a generation of business owners that lenders were in the market for taking risks. Many businesses before the crisis were getting finance at below sustainable rates and for the wrong reasons, chiefly because of the price of their owners' home rather than the viability of their business idea. When reality dawned on the financial markets, these companies had their credit lines cut off along with the rest of the market. The difference was that many of these businesses, without viable business models, deserved it.

What the flood of money made available during the good times also did was encourage people to load up with funding before embarking on their entrepreneurial journey. This was also a tragedy because starting with little funding is what many rebel entrepreneurs will tell you is the best way to start a business. In fact, taking outside money from a bank or venture capital firm may be the worst thing you can do to a fledgling enterprise.

The case for bootstrapping

Neville Wright founded Kiddicare in 1974 with his wife Marilyn as a small baby equipment shop in a street in Peterborough, in the east of England. For years the business trundled along, occasionally moving location, but doing nothing that needed outside financial help. The Wrights's daughter Elaine then married Scott Weaver and they became the Weaver-Wrights. Scott was a dab hand with technology and a new way of trading goods, called the world wide web, had come along, so Scott decided to put Kiddicare online.

In three years, the business had grown 75 per cent and in February 2011 Morrisons, the UK's fourth biggest supermarket chain, bought

Kiddicare for £70 m. By this point, Kiddicare was employing about 130 people and was the largest privately owned nursery supplier in the country, shipping 150,000 items a month. Iain Crighton, Chairman of Peterborough Chamber of Commerce, said at the time: 'It's that sort of success story people love to hear about.'

What most people did not talk about was that Kiddicare did not have a penny in debt.

As enterprise correspondent for the *Financial Times*, covering small business issues, I have received more than my fair share of heartbreaking stories from business owners since the financial crisis struck. They have often been cut off by their banks for what seems like no better reason than that the board have decided certain companies or industries are not worth continuing to support. Without these funds, many businesses struggle to get by, leading to anger at their lenders.

However, the issue is rarely as simple as the stereotype of greedy bank bosses refusing to provide money to otherwise viable businesses. The problem is often that companies are too willing to get themselves into debt when a better business plan that was better executed would not have needed it.

A little discussed point is that most businesses in many developed countries do not go to the bank manager for a loan. According to the most comprehensive study of the UK small business market, compiled by Warwick Business School's Centre for Small and Medium-Sized Enterprises (SMEs), only 24.3 per cent of companies with 250 or fewer staff had term loans between 2001 and 2004. In 2008–09 this fell to just 11.4 per cent of these companies. Overdrafts are more popular, but are still a minority pursuit. Only 41.5 per cent of businesses in the Warwick Business School survey had these in 2008–09, slightly less than the 42.5 per cent that had them between 2005 and 2008. Many of the start-ups interviewed by Warwick's researchers chose to max out on their credit cards to get their ideas off the ground.

It is not even a case of entrepreneurs refusing loans because the bank is only offering the money on punitive terms, although this does happen. The fact is that, while many good companies have been frustrated in their pursuit of bank finance, many more have either given up or look to other means to grow their business. The most common means of finance for start-up companies is the people closest at hand – a rich uncle or former work colleague who rates you as a person and likes your idea. It is what is often abbreviated to the 3Fs – friends, family and fools.

The myth, perpetuated by business groups whose members are angry about the banks and reality television entrepreneurship pro-grammes that understand the pulling power of a big cash prize, is that all great businesses start with a large dollop of outside money. In fact, some of the most successful companies of recent years were started with little more than a good idea, some space in the spare room and a lot of hard work.

A good example of this is Jamie Murray Wells, founder of online spectacle retailer Glasses Direct. His company, now based in stylish warehouse offices around the back of London's Oxford Street, is built on a cunningly disruptive business model made all the more lucrative and scalable by the internet age.

It starts with the fact that British opticians must, by law, provide people with free eye tests. Your average high-street eye specialist overcomes this piece of well-meaning red tape by cross-subsidizing the cost of the eye tests they have to provide by charging customers that need glasses more than the market rate for their lenses.

At the frighteningly young age of 20, Jamie saw the opportunity to undercut the industry by offering to take the prescriptions cus-tomers have got for free from their optician and selling them lenses online for cost price. Since he was not an optician, there was no obligation for him to provide eye tests. In fact, without a physical presence on the high street, there was no way Jamie could provide eye tests even if he wanted to. However, it did mean he could sell glasses to people at a considerable discount to what was then available.

Even with a small margin on top, Jamie calculated that he could give people new spectacles for a tenth of the price on the British high street. Using the internet as a distribution mechanism, meaning that he did not need to own physical stores, enabled Jamie to keep the price for the customer down even further.

The only hitch was that Jamie was at the time a penniless student, still finishing his degree at the University of the West of England in Bristol. However, he did not let a small matter of having no money get in the way of him getting his big idea off the ground.

I am not sure whether, being a student, Jamie would have got the time of day from his bank manager, but he did not turn to this option for a conventional term loan. He did not even go to the bank of mum and dad, although, as has already been noted with regard to the 3Fs, this is a popular route for many founders. No, Jamie had an even better source of seed finance for his business in the form of the last instalment of his student loan. This was money the British government had been supplying to university students at below market rates, or even free if you do not earn sufficient amounts after graduating, ever since it did away with the country's higher education grant system in the early 1990s.

The beauty of this sort of debt funding source for Jamie was that he did not need to prepare a pitch to angel investors or even draw up a business plan for his bank manager to get the money. He merely had to sign a few forms and the cash was his.

Since those early days, when Jamie and a few friends sat stuffing envelopes with spectacles around his parents' kitchen table, the business has grown rapidly. Glasses Direct is now the world's largest purely online retailer of spectacles and contact lenses. In order to fuel this rapid ascent, the company has since raised several rounds of funding from private investors and venture capital firms, but the fact remains that it was able to start with a government loan of just a few hundred pounds.

I must state that the point of this chapter is not to dismiss conventional debt or equity finance, but to say that starting a business with the few resources you yourself can muster is actually a good way to give a great business a good start in life, for reasons we will come onto later.

There is, of course, a word for this process of setting up with next to nothing, using the various free services available to business and eking every last penny out of your available resources – and that word is bootstrapping. It is a rather clumsy word, but useful shorthand for the process of pulling yourself up by your bootstraps.

The practice is as old as the hills. However, the emergence of the web as a route to market, supported by powerful but very cheap computer-processing power to run back office functions, has made starting a company nowadays a lot cheaper and has therefore made bootstrapping a much more talked about process.

It was Gordon Moore, co-founder of chipmaker Intel, who was credited with spotting in the 1960s that the amount of inexpensive computer-processing power that could be fitted on a circuit board was roughly doubling every two years. This rapid evolution of processing power was further aided by the creation of the world wide web as a free depository for information and commerce in the early 1990s. Technological developments, such as fast broadband internet connections and cloud computing (the IT equivalent of moving electricity production to a national grid), have only accelerated the process of lowering the cost of starting a business, at least in the developed world.

All this has meant that start-ups reliant on technology, of which there are many, have found it less and less expensive to begin trading. All Jamie needed to get Glasses Direct started was a supplier of lenses, a decent website and space at home to pack and dispatch the orders.

Small is beautiful, at least to begin with

Of course, if you only have a little money, you will have to start small. The point is to look at this as an advantage, not a problem. Jamie is very clear about this. He told me his personal philosophy was: start small, grow big; start big, go bust. 'There is a bit of a stigma to starting up from the garage or the living room but it is the only way to minimize the risk before you pull in a whole lot of money,' he explained.

Another graduate entrepreneur, who has gone even further than Jamie in building a global brand, is Peter Williams, founder of the British preppy fashion label Jack Wills. Peter, a ginger-haired bespectacled economics graduate, claims that his friends wet themselves laughing when he suggested to them that he would create a clothing fashion business. However, 11 years later, with sales of £135 m and earnings before interest, tax depreciation and amortization of £25 m, most people take Peter seriously. And all this has been achieved with a single investment of £40,000, made up of Peter's personal savings, an inheritance, an overdraft and several maxed-out credit cards.

Although Peter sold a stake in the business in 2007 in order to buy a house for his wife and newly born child, Jack Wills has needed no additional cash injection to fund its growth beyond that first six-figure sum. That is a pretty amazing achievement when you think about it, which is one of the reasons why Peter can be considered a rebel entrepreneur.

Of course, bootstrapping like this meant that Peter and his business partner and university friend Robert Shaw had to make some quite harsh economies during the early days of the business. This included sleeping above their first shop in the secluded Devon sailing town of Salcombe in order to keep down costs. For two years they lived off 'onion surprise', a recipe whose only other ingredient (apart from the eponymous garden bulb) was Bisto gravy granules, according to Peter.

The founders' genius move was to create an exclusivity to the brand among its 16–21-year-old target market, such that it becomes known to most of its customers through word-of-mouth recommendation. Marketing for Jack Wills is limited to social networking sites and sponsorship of events where its target market congregates. Even the shops tend to be off the beaten track, situated for the most part where young people tend to hang out rather than prime city locations.

This not only means that customers are more loyal when they find out about Jack Wills, Peter claims, but it saves the company a large chunk of money on property, advertising and marketing bills. Whereas luxury fashion labels on average allocate 10 per cent of their sales revenue to advertising and marketing their image, Jack Wills spends just half of 1 per cent, allowing the rest to flow to the bottom line.

The value of having no money

Bootstrapping a business is not easy, particularly in the early years, and Jack Wills was no exception. The business made a measly £56,000 in revenue in its first year, barely improving on this amount in the next 12 months.

However, its focus on keeping costs down, and therefore having to think more cleverly than other fashion retailers, led to innovations that have enabled the company to grow faster in its maturity. This is the real value of bootstrapping. The lack of funding forces you to innovate, but you cannot waste money that you do not have, so you make every penny count. Jack Wills is now on the leading edge of multichannel retailing, with a quarter of its sales coming through online shoppers.

This was partly due to the good fortune of starting in 1999 at the height of the dotcom boom without the baggage that other traditional retailers had in terms of shops to service. However, the innovations the company has created in selling were also born out of the necessity of having no spare cash. When Jack Wills opened its second store, in the equally out-of-the-way location of Aldeburgh, Suffolk, Robert was packed off to live nearby in a beaten-up old caravan borrowed from a friend. This money-saving measure subsequently became part of the charm of the Jack Wills brand. Robert, the man in the caravan, created the space where all the coolest local kids got their polo shirts, cargo pants and tweed jackets.

The point was that, being constantly limited by resources, Robert and Peter had to think creatively. The Aldeburgh shop was an old petrol station, which still had the original pumps in the forecourt. 'This led to a second movement of hilarity from our friends, who said we would sell cigarettes and porn mags,' Peter recalled in a talk he gave at a luxury brands conference held in the *Financial Times* in 2011. 'Quite frankly I would have done anything to make money.' With Jack Wills now open in the United States and aiming to take a $1 m share of the market, Paul will probably not now need to resort to such tactics.

That original £40,000 has certainly been made to work hard, but having to work within a tight budget has helped create a world-beating brand with real strength.

Contrast Jack Wills with the many dotcom ventures started around the same time that Peter got going in 1999, pumped full of private equity money like a goose being made into foie gras, only to burst spectacularly shortly afterwards. Boo.com, the fashion website, started trading in the same year as Jack Wills with an incredible $135 m of venture capital backing. Within 18 months it was insolvent, having spent all of that incredible mountain of cash.

The way Jack Wills has financed itself has meant that Paul still maintains a majority stake in his creation. As a result, he does not need to talk a lot about his company and can focus on long-term planning to make Jack Wills even stronger for the future.

Have you tried the alternatives to the bank?

One of the most common complaints I receive from business owners is that banks do not seem to want to help them. What they often mean is that the banks they have visited have not been willing to give money that they might see as working capital but the lending institution views as risk capital.

There is no doubt that dealing with banks has become more difficult in recent years. Even without the financial crisis, the trend towards centralizing decision making has undermined whatever bond of trust existed between company owners and their local bank branch manager. However, the banks have a point to make too. They claim, with some justification, that the owner-managers often only go to their bank when they need the cash, often at a moment of crisis. If they only maintained a regular dialogue with their lender, the banking executives argue, the branch manager could be more under-standing of the company's position.

The blame game, however, rarely gets anyone anywhere. The reality is that, in the years running up to the point where the banking industry was brought to its knees, there was too much money being lent by the major financial institutions to companies at unsustainable market rates on the basis of an owner's rising house price rather than solid business propositions. Since then the pendulum has swung the other way with a large degree of over caution, and inflated loan rates to match.

This raises the question of whether you should put such reliance on a lender in the first place. Many companies are trying to square the issue by cutting their costs to preserve cash. We will return to the dangers of such a strategy later in this book.

While there is no doubt that a large equity investment or bank loan can add rocket boosters to a company's growth prospects, it is equally true that it is possible to generate substantial growth for an enterprise without significant amounts of external money. There is some evidence for this.

Another UK academic study, in 2009, concluded that the secret to consistently fast business growth was actually to not resort to venture capital funding and to avoid diluting the founders' equity stakes. Using a sample of 7,203 companies, the researchers separated out about 10 per cent that could be described as fast-growing 'gazelle' businesses at some point in their existence. However, only a small fraction of these gazelles were able to maintain their growth levels above 30 per cent over a period of five years.

When the strategies of these gazelle businesses were analysed, they actually differed little from the slower-growing businesses, although the former were more likely to have a marketing department.

The one thing that was consistent among those that could maintain gazelle-like rates of growth over the medium term was that they were least likely to sell shares in the business to others, such as directors, employees or venture capital firms.

The findings suggest people who own fast-growing businesses are more likely to want to hold onto all the fruits of their hard work, which is not surprising perhaps. However, it is heartening that they are also able to achieve this dream while building fast-growing companies.

Some successful entrepreneurs believe that the venture capital model is broken and that entrepreneurs should fund everything themselves. One of the leading advocates of this approach is Bill Liao, a serial entrepreneur, who founded the social networking website Xing. 'It is a rare equity investor indeed who can give good counsel without diluting the core innovation of the start-up entrepreneurs,' he told me. 'They demand big equity to come on board, yet my experience is the more they demand up front the more dilutive of progress their opinions are, and the more unproductive they make the whole team.'

Bill is so passionate in his belief about the need to finance yourself that he wrote a book about the subject, called *Stone Soup*. You may know the folk story from which the book title comes, about a storyteller who arrives in a famine-stricken village. He has no raw ingredients, but has a stone and a pot to cook with. He puts down his pot, fills it with water, places the stone inside and lights a fire underneath to heat it. The storyteller then starts doing what he does best, telling stories, and invites others to contribute food in return, adding what they have to the pot. The result is that everyone is fed.

Bill became a multimillionaire from his business ideas and now spends a lot of his time involved in philanthropy and charity work. He claims that the most important point is not what you have but knowing what you want to achieve. If you have this goal then it is all a matter of achieving it, he claims.

Bill starts his story in 1994 when he was 27, married, working for a computer company in his native Australia and A$30,000 in debt. His wife went to a talk held by a charity called the Hunger Project, and came home inspired by the work it was doing in the developing world. 'She came back with a light in her eyes and said, "Bill, you have to go and visit this,"' he told me. 'It is not just a charity.'

He went and was challenged by a director of the charity to come up with a donation of A$50,000. He tried explaining his dire financial circumstances, but she refused to be swayed. 'She asked me who I would have to become and what I would have to change in order for that to happen,' Bill recalled. 'I realized in that moment that I would need that to happen.'

Bill did do something. Something very radical, in fact.

He quit his job, studied the art of closing deals and launched his first business teaching engineers how to sell. Becoming a serial entrepreneur, his first wealth arrived when he sold that business for A$500,000. Although he had still not repaid all his debts, Bill gave A$100,000 of the proceeds to the Hunger Project. He then pledged to become a millionaire by the time he was 30. 'In the end, I had to wait until I was 31,' he said.

Bill eventually achieved his goal after becoming director of operations at Davnet, a telecommunications company that achieved the fastest capital value growth in the history of the Australian Stock Exchange. The wealth gave him the freedom to pursue his charitable goals.

However, he admits his riches were initially a burden. 'Money is toxic,' he told me. 'It wrecks your head. I made 10 or 15 investments that all went south. The only thing that saved me was that I had these other noble causes.'

Xing was one of his subsequent successes. Bill co-founded the business with Lars Hinrichs, a German entrepreneur, and they sold it to achieve Bill's third big cash accumulation in 2006.

Bill has now been involved in seven initial public offerings and is chief executive of Finaxis, a privately held financial services business. He is also helping 33 start-ups, but he prefers to contribute his knowledge rather than money.

'I am sick of getting friendly-looking e-mails that end up with a request for a $50,000 investment,' he told me. 'I will put small amounts into companies but I prefer to give my support. All the cash from venture capital firms just attracts bozos and gives companies terrible valuations that they cannot fulfil.'

Bill's philanthropic ventures include the WeForest Movement, a charity that aims to battle global warming by planting 2,000 billion trees in the next decade. Among its schemes is a corporate tree-planting plan called 'Buy Two Get One Tree'. 'If Coke planted a tree for every can of drink it sold, we could reforest the planet in three years,' he said.

Bill is an example of the power of thought. His philosophy might sound extreme but in many ways it is no different from that of any entrepreneur, starting out with nothing but an idea and a vague notion of how to get there. The point is that money followed Bill's entrepreneurial ambitions. It did not lead it.

Pull yourself up by your bootstraps

Bill's success is owed in no small part to the efficiencies created by the internet and Moore's Law that I have spoken about already.

This is probably why bootstrapping has become something of a mantra in the technology industry, even among venture capitalists. Davor Hebel, a partner at Fidelity Growth Partners Europe, a private equity operation in London, is a fan of the phenomenon. 'We love bootstrapped entrepreneurs because as a rule they demonstrate sophistication, rigour and tenacity,' he told me. 'By definition they tend to grow slower than their funded counterparts and are often built on more solid foundations, given their need to be super-efficient from day one. Once these bootstrapped success stories gain access to growth capital, we often find they are the ones that outperform their peers.'

The good news is that it is possible to achieve considerable success through your own resources, cleverly managing the money coming into your business, even getting it in before you have to pay suppliers, and using commercial partners to finance your expansion.

Bootstrapping is less common in the centuries-old industry of making food than the more 21st-century industry of internet-based businesses. However, it does occur there too. One pair of entrepreneurs who told me that they passionately believed in avoiding term loans from the banks, and outside equity finance for that matter, were Praveen Vijh and Preet Grewal, the founders of Eat Natural, a manufacturer of healthy cereal bars.

The former school friends from Essex met me for a coffee at the foodie haven of Borough Market in central London. They told me that their main driver in business was the quality of their product rather than clever leveraging instruments.

The pair had formed Eat Natural because they saw a gap in the market for high-quality snacks that, in Praveen's words, 'do not taste like sawdust'. Despite the lack of outside finance (Eat Natural was started with £30,000 of personal savings), the founders retain control over the whole manufacturing process. They own all their factories, or 'makeries' as they call them, where all the cereal bars are hand-made.

It took Eat Natural's team 13 years of hard work, but the business in 2010 sold some £35m of cereal bars, one-fifth of which are exported. It now sells its wares in more than 30 countries.

Taking bank debt might have enabled Eat Natural to grow faster, but both the founders believe it would have been a more risky move. 'It is not that we have a problem with bank finance – it is more to do with the fact that we want to grow sustainably,' Praveen told me. 'We do not want to try to run before we can walk.'

A case in point was in 2000, when the business was approached with an order for millions of its bars by Sam's Club, a chain of membership-only warehouse stores in the United States that is owned and operated by Walmart, the world's largest supermarket group. The offer was highly tempting to Eat Natural's team, which at the time had not signed up a big retailer in their home market. Praveen and Preet told me that they spent three months negotiating with Sam's Club's European office in Florence, a considerable drain on their time and resources given that they were both still heavily involved in day-to-day operations.

The deal collapsed, however, because it would have meant increasing the company's production facilities fivefold, an investment the founders could not make without outside finance. 'On the one hand, it could have gone very well and transformed the business, but it would have meant risking everything,' Praveen explained. 'We just weren't willing to take that risk.'

With hindsight, it was a smart decision – not least because accepting the deal would have made Eat Natural reliant on one customer for 80 per cent of its total sales.

Soon after Eat Natural rejected Sam's Club, they struck a deal with Tesco, the world's third largest supermarket group and the largest player in Eat Natural's home market, the UK. Sainsbury's, the British number three, then came on board. The business was able to satisfy these orders within existing cash flow, enabling it to remain profitable while growing at 40 to 50 per cent a year. Eat Natural's 140 staff made over 4 million bars a month in 2010, and the business did it without the need to seek outside finance.

In 2009, the company had enough free cash to spend close to £1 m upgrading its packing equipment lines while putting another £2 m into advertising. By avoiding debt finance, the owners of Eat Natural boast that they are free to make decisions like this without thinking how they are going to meet loan repayments to the bank. Perhaps the biggest risk for the business now is not financing, but the ability of the company to expand beyond its core product.

Preet and Praveen have since made a move into toasted cereals, which was something of a departure for them.

'For us, the business has always been about building it in steps,' Preet said.

What founders like Preet and Praveen often talk about is the sustainability of their business. Not over-leveraging yourself with someone else's money is often part of this process.

The Draft House is a small chain of pubs, specializing in high-quality independent beers that are not available in the larger pub chains. The founder, Charlie McVeigh – a former financial consultant and business journalist who had already started and sold a nightclub, a restaurant and a pub business – believes he has created a way of turning a profit from drinking holes in out-of-the-way locations, such as his site in Battersea, by offering something people cannot get elsewhere. 'I meant to get out of the business, but I found I could not give it up,' he told me. 'It is a bad habit but one that gives me some satisfaction.'

The problem Charlie had was that he had already tried and failed with a concept for his Battersea pub, and all the banks he approached felt this made it too much of a risk. As a result, Charlie was forced to survive on his own resources, using money he had made on his previous ventures. 'It forced us to focus on being profitable and cash-generative as a single site operation,' he told me. 'This teaches you what is possible in terms of revenue and costs.'

The pictures on the walls of his pub are a prime example of how needing to save money can create a unique character for a business, Charlie said. The £150,000 he spent fitting out the place was less than a third of the cost he would have had to pay outside decorators, he claims, and provided a good return on the £200,000 a year that the site now brings in.

Charlie also kept his staff costs down by offering employees a room above the pub as a part of the pay package. But it was not just about cost-cutting. One innovation was to allow ales to be bought by the third of a pint. This was good for revenue because it encouraged customers to spend money when they might have thought a beer too expensive. It also helped with cash flow.

The lack of spare cash has meant that the business has had to create a more robust business model, Charlie insisted. 'It means that we can take pub sites that are failing and for no money or very little money we can make them look cool,' he told me.

Another evangelist for bootstrapping is Harry Clarke. He saved money when starting his transport technology business, Cobalt, by operating out of a temporary workspace, called a portakabin. From here, his team developed Ring Go, a method of paying car-parking charges over mobile phones that has since been adopted by more than 100 local authorities across the UK, generating revenues of more than £1 m. Despite its rapid growth, Harry has been able to retain complete control over the brand without a penny of outside funding.

Harry believes that bootstrapping forces you to have a tight strategic focus, but enables you to make decisions quickly and easily because there are no outside shareholders to answer to. 'A culture of frugality is ground in, and every decision is made for cash reasons.'

Another believer in the value of growing from your own resources is Jonathan Grey, founder and managing director of Ovation Incentives, which provides companies with corporate gift vouchers to encourage customers to spend more and motivate staff. 'Self-funding makes your business strategy a marathon, not a sprint,' he said.

David Molian is a lecturer in entrepreneurship at Cranfield University, a college in the English Midlands that created the Business Growth and Development Programme (BGP), a practical course aimed specifically at enabling ambitious entrepreneurs to look inside themselves, with the help of mentors and other owner-managers, to find ways to accelerate their growth. BGP has become a key staging post for over 1,250 British founders since it was set up in 1988, partly because there is little else like this on the market in the UK, but also because it is rare to get the opportunity to take time away from your business and immerse yourself in the company of fellow entrepreneurs. Cranfield's extensive list of BGP alumni also gives it an authority to speak about the issues affecting UK entrepreneurs.

David told me that most successful owner-managers on BGP warn against parting with equity early unless absolutely necessary. The exception, he said, is the use of equity to tie in key people once the business is established. 'Most successful entrepreneurs I know have gone down this route. Some even insist that key people have an equity stake in the business.'

A few years ago, some of the team at BGP set up a similar course, called Your Business Your Future (YBYF) at the Cass Business School, part of City University in London. Gerard Burke, YBYF founder, backs up the BGP findings. He claims that 90 per cent of the people that his team teaches are self-funded. This is partly because of the nature of most businesses and the managers that run them, he told me. Businesses tend to be based on the particular skill, capability or network of the original founder and have a limited ability to reach the sort of scale that equity investors would typically seek. Owner-managers often run their own businesses because they have high needs for autonomy and control, too. 'Having an external investor is perceived as giving up some of that autonomy and control, and most owner-managers simply don't want to do that,' Gerard said.

If you can't get a loan, get a grant

One way to avoid recourse to the bank or a venture capital firm is to obtain a grant. This is what Evan Rudowski and Miles Galliford did when they launched Sub Hub, a software company that enables other budding entrepreneurs to create commercial membership websites of their own.

The pair relocated from London to Cardiff Bay to take advantage of the grants, low-interest loans and other subsidies available in Wales, which have made up £330,000 of Sub Hub's initial funding. Evan, a New Yorker by birth, explained to me that Cardiff was a far cheaper place to be based in than the Big Apple.

Being located in the Welsh capital also allowed the company to stand out from the crowd in a way that it would not have done in the city that never sleeps or London, where Evan and Miles have spent time. 'In Cardiff Bay, we are one of the hottest companies, whereas in London we would be competing with many others for the best talent,' Evan explained.

The Welsh Assembly also subsidized trade missions for Sub Hub to the United States. Partly as a result of this, 70 per cent of Sub Hub's customer base comes from the United States.

One of the advantages of taking public money instead of private is that you are not under such pressure to produce a quick return, Evan told me. This was valuable for Sub Hub, which has changed its business model several times since Evan and Miles quit their jobs to start the company in 2004. 'We have had a cushion to make mistakes and learn from them,' Evan said.

Timing can be everything

Sometimes, successful self-financing is a matter of timing.

When Ross Hugo launched Holidaylets.net in January 2003, the market for renting holiday homes online was white-hot. He started with 500 properties on his website and increased this to 11,000 properties in four years, using his own resources. 'It was a bit of a land grab,' he told me. In 2007 Ross sold to his much larger French rival, Homelidays, for several million pounds, shortly before his purchaser itself became the target of a takeover by the main US player, Home-away.com.

Ross admitted to me that he might have grown faster and bigger with private equity cash behind him. However, he said he doubted whether the outcome would have been any different. 'The Americans do it on such a grand scale. I don't think people would have taken us seriously enough to lend us the kind of money we'd need to compete with that.'

Once again it is Moore's Law and the ever decreasing price of technology that give a helping hand to companies such as Sub Hub and Holidaylets.net. This does make self-funding a lot more easy. In the dotcom boom of the 1990s it would have cost a Silicon Valley technology start-up several million dollars to buy all the servers necessary to set up a retail website. Today the necessary power can be bought for a fraction of the price.

We are all dotcoms now, thank goodness

Such economies are not so obvious if you are the head of a clothing business, like Michael Conway at the Quayside Group. However, he too has moved online.

The business started off as a fashion import company that supplied garments to high-street retailers, such as Next, House of Fraser and C&A. The day before Michael was due to complete a £750,000 management buyout of the business – which he was running at the time for a large textile manufacturer – the venture capitalists backing the deal rang to say they were withdrawing their funding. Michael went ahead with the deal regardless, saddling himself with £80,000 of personal debt, and kept the company afloat through asset and debtor finance from a trade finance company. 'I put in pretty much everything I had,' he told me.

However, this gave him the freedom to remake the business model completely, reinventing the company as an online supplier of clothing for workwear, promotions and events. The business expanded to trade under the websites clothes2order.com, polo-shirts.co.uk and safclothing.com, and boasts the Virgin Group and the BBC among its clients.

Between 2008 and 2009, immediately after the financial crisis struck, revenue at the Quayside Group increased by 70 per cent to £3.9 m. Moreover, because customers paid when they placed the order, rather than when they received the goods, the Quayside Group generated a positive cash flow and no longer needed its debt facilities.

'We have no limit on expansion through our own finances,' Michael told me. At the time, he was about to buy a second large distribution centre. Three banks and various private individuals had offered him funding to expand the business, but Michael had declined them all. 'Short-term, day-to-day borrowing with a bank is fine, but be careful in your financial arrangements that you do not become reliant on a facility that can be pulled at any moment,' he said.

No man is an island when it comes to funding

For all the benefits of bootstrapping and growth financed through cash flow, there does come a point for many fast-growing companies where outside support may well be needed.

Bruce Greig built his first business, an online tradesperson service called 0800Handyman, with about £100,000 of angel investment, but then sold it for more than £1m in 2007 while still a majority shareholder. His next venture, Keep Me Booked, a web-based software system designed for guesthouses, B&Bs and small hotels, had just reached break-even on £65,000 when I spoke to him. That was about 1 per cent of the amount his main UK rival has raised from its venture capital backers, he said.

Bruce boasted to me that in both these cases he had kept the level of outside funding to a minimum, partly because of the discipline this instils when growing the business. 'If you raise lots of money, you have to spend it,' he said. 'If you don't have lots of money, you are forced to be lean so you reach breakeven sooner.'

After two years of building the Draft House on his own resources, Charlie McVeigh raised £900,000 in March 2009 to open two more sites in central London. He told me when I came across him in 2011 that he would now like to add some bank debt to expand his chain further. So, while he told me that he remained a believer in the value of funding everything yourself, he admitted that there was a need for outside money to sustain growth. 'Excessive dilution destroys founder motivation, but a loss of momentum will cause you to lose key staff,' he said.

It may come as a surprise that many successful entrepreneurs actually turn down offers of finance from outsiders. George Bevis turned down 'two very prominent' angel investors for his young internet business Speedsell, which buys and resells video game consoles for people. 'The offer was rubbish, the terms were absolutely absurd,' George told me, noting that too many people, especially at the moment, will grab the first offer they get. He insisted that it was the right choice for him but admitted that it was an easier decision to make because he was looking for 'tens of thousands of pounds', instead of the millions of pounds that some start-ups believe they need. His aim was to use the extra funds to increase working capital so Speedsell could grow faster.

'We buy items from customers but we resell them later so, for a week or two, we have to fund ownership of the stock,' he said.

George knows a bit about the value of money, having worked for several years as a banker at RBS, nurturing his personal business venture in his spare time. He put about £100,000 of his personal savings and wages into Speedsell before quitting his day job the Friday before the collapse of Lehman Brothers sent the banking sector into a tailspin.

According to George, the angel investors he came across were too greedy in their valuations of his fledgling venture. 'With an early-stage investor, it is very important that you have someone who will be your friend. If they are trying to show off to you on terms up front, then they are just not acting in the right way.'

George was better able than some early-stage entrepreneurs to say no to outside funding because he was not desperate for large sums of cash. Although he had no rich family members to help him, he was able to raise the money he wanted by tapping various personal contacts. 'Frankly, if you are an entrepreneur who cannot find a rich person to help you out, then you are not going to get anywhere,' he told me.

Cases like Speedsell are exceptional, according to those in the venture capital (VC) business, who have found themselves in the happy position of being able to call the shots when it comes to investment as bank funding has dried up.

Not that they are rushing into deals. Pi Capital, an investor network, has turned down a number of investments in recent years. David Giampaolo, Pi Capital's chief executive, told me that many of these proposals were 'just no good'. The rest might be interesting, but the entrepreneurs concerned have unrealistic expectations. 'Sometimes you need to be more focused on return of capital rather than return on capital,' he told me, noting that he would rather keep money in a low-interest bank account when the economic situation makes future performance of any business so difficult to gauge.

Many successful entrepreneurs see the world differently, though. Simon Campbell, who went to 25 outside venture capital firms before launching his innovative mail business ViaPost, claims that there is often a conflict between the aims of venture capital firms and ambitious owners of growing businesses. 'VCs love smart-looking business plans, and a level of forecasting detail that is not really appropriate for a start-up,' he told me.

The problem with raising early-stage backing for ViaPost, which turns computer documents into physical mail, was that potential investors were insisting on a proof of concept before the service went live. 'That wasn't reasonable,' according to Simon, who ended up raising £450,000 from a private investor and his chairman.

After successfully launching his service in 2007, Simon raised another £600,000 from angel networks. Despite what might be considered appalling timing, given the state of the global economy, he had raised all he wanted just a few months later.

Simon did attract the attention of one venture capital firm during that funding round, but turned it down. 'They procrastinated a little bit and we said, "don't bother". My attitude now is: you weren't there when we were early stage so why would we want you now?'

The decision to turn down outside investors is often more of an emotional choice than one based on economics, according to Gerard Burke at YBYF. 'There is a mindset issue about private equity,' he said. 'The vast majority of people are in business because, at least in part, they have strong needs for autonomy and control – so when they look at private equity taking part ownership, they see a loss of autonomy and a loss of control.'

Mary Pratt, founder of Norwich-based recruitment business Cocoabean, told me that there were good reasons for guarding such autonomy: to retain the culture of her company and enact new strategies quickly. 'With recruitment, you don't need a massive investment. Your investment is your staff,' she said. 'I have seen business owners see the pound signs before their eyes, take the money and regretted it.'

It was the 18th-century, London-born poet Alexander Pope who coined the observation that fools rush in where angels fear to tread.

In the case of Conversocial, a very 21st-century London-based social networking marketing support service, it was friends and family doing all the rushing before angels (wealthy private individuals) arrive on the scene with their cash. Joshua March, Conversocial's founder, had followed the route of many early-stage entrepreneurs by tapping relatives and associates for some seed funding. In his case, a cousin put down several thousand pounds to get the business idea off the ground – in return for what seemed like great terms for the entrepreneur. Only they weren't.

An anti-dilution clause had been inserted into the contract, which seemed fair enough at the time but caused grief when Joshua went to raise his first significant round of funding from outside investors a few years later. 'It wasn't a purposeful thing,' Joshua told me, defending his cousin's position. 'I didn't know better and neither did my family member.'

What this tale shows is that the process of fundraising is fraught with potential problems and can trip up even the most well-meaning individuals and their associates.

Sue Acton, who took voluntary redundancy from Barclays, spent six months raising £33,000 for her venture, Bubbles & Balm – the UK's first 100 per cent Fairtrade body care products maker. Her first backer was a former colleague at Barclays. Her second came through Angels Den, a private investor introduction service that charges lower fees than traditional angel networks. Sue's third angel was completely random – a person who happened to be sitting in the audience at a talk she was giving on marketing at Warwick University.

With hindsight, Sue told me that she wished she had sought more money from her first three angels, having since discovered that the process of fundraising is just as time-consuming, no matter how much cash you are after.

When I spoke to her in 2011 she was on her second round of fundraising, this time using crowd funding, a process by which companies use the internet to reach a large audience of what can be very small-scale backers. This kind of peer-to-peer lending is another way the internet has helped to reduce the cost of getting a business going.

One thing Sue said she had learnt was the need to be prepared to walk away from deals if investors were too greedy or want to steer the business idea too far from its original plan. 'One guy was very keen to invest but wanted me to move into the Far East,' she recalled. 'I was not averse to that, but I felt at this stage, and for the amount of money I was looking for, I needed to grow [the business] in this country first.'

Simon Prockter now has three technology-driven start-ups under his belt, his third being a home dining service called Housebites, where professional restaurant chefs cook for delivery to the houses of foodies in London. When I spoke to him, he had secured two rounds of fundraising for Housebites, using the experience gained through his previous ventures to persuade three wealthy backers to stump up cash. Experience does not make the process easier, however, he told me. It took him six months of solid work to secure his money for Housebites, little different from funding rounds for previous ventures.

'The second you start fundraising you have to focus on that alone,' he told me. 'It prevents you from running your business, when ultimately it is the business that will get you the traction that will get you the big round [of funding].'

The first few pitches of any fundraising round are destined to end in failure because of the long odds of finding the right investor, he added. Simon's advice, however, is to treat the knock-backs as a learning exercise. 'Ask yourself: "Why did they say no? What do we have to do to change the business plan?"'

For Housebites, Simon tried angel networks and publicly funded programmes, both of which he found had shortcomings. However, he admitted that founders would be foolish not to at least try these avenues.

Simon ended up with a mix of investors: a banker, a management consultant and a serial entrepreneur. The entrepreneur is a friend who had invested in his ventures before. 'I had this idea and told him, and he agreed to become an investor there and then.' Having him on board helped give Simon credibility when seeking to attract other backers. Investment bankers make good angels, and they have money, Simon noted. 'These guys are natural-born investors,' he said.

There is evidently a difference, therefore, between what bankers will do with their own money and their company's cash.

The biggest problem for Simon was pinning his banker down to get a deal out of him. 'He was a trader and I couldn't talk to him in office hours.'

The management consultant came through a third party. 'I met a hedge fund manager at a party,' Simon said. 'He didn't have the money but he knew a guy.'

But there are other types of angel and other routes to finding them. Simon recommended researching people who have recently benefited from business exits and trying to find people you know who can provide connections to these people. His other tip was to make sure that you have a big celebration the night you sign the deal with your angels. 'Go out and have a glass of champagne, because the next day those angels will be on the phone asking about the business.'

The US technology industry makes a great play about the amount of equity capital available to start-ups. But it is important to get the right investment from the right sort of investor at the right time. Those within the Silicon Valley scene also stress that the money is not as important as the people behind it, who can guide the founders through the inevitable slings and arrows of building an enterprise.

Californian John Hering is one of the Silicon Valley entrepreneurial team behind LookOut Mobile, whose security software is doing for smartphones what Symantec and McAfee did for personal computers a decade before. John, the son of two business owners, was displaying a canny sense of the commercial at an early age. When he was sent out to paint the kerb white outside his parent's California home John figured that his neighbours might well want the service – for some reason, many local governments in the state do not pay to maintain the edges of residential streets. He went round the town and soon had orders worth $10,000, not bad for a schoolboy. He was soon using the money to build his own stock portfolio.

This kind of ingenuity may explain why investors were so willing to take a punt on John and his fellow founders.

LookOut Mobile was formed with the help of $5 m in seed funding from Vinod Khosla, one of the founders of Sun Microsystems, a Silicon Valley success story of a previous generation. Eighteen months later, during which time the company had gone from 10 staff and 100,000 customers to 100 staff and 13 million customers, LookOut Mobile's team raised another $20 m from Index Ventures, a private equity firm that specializes in early-stage investments.

These kinds of sums are fantastic to many founders, but John insisted to me that the money was secondary to the real prize of such equity rounds – the brains of the people putting forward the money. 'These guys were wonderful,' he eulogized. Vinod, John explained, was key at the time in holding the hands of him and his co-founders in the early days of the business.

Index, which has offices in San Francisco, London and Geneva, was a good fit for LookOut Media, given its plan was to expand internationally. The UK and Japan are now two of its key markets.

'It is all about finding the right investor at the right stage,' John said to me. Just as a good equity backer can provide the kind of guidance necessary to take a business to the next level, the wrong person can be poison, no matter how much cash they are putting in. It can even be a case of the right private equity firm but the wrong partner, John added. 'Having a great firm is important, but the board member, for me, is more important than anything else.'

Few people these days could expect to be called up by their bank manager asking for business. However, Alan O'Brien, chief executive of Sabien Technology, took a call from the boss himself at his bank, Barclays, when John Varley, its then chief executive, rang to ask about Sabien's energy-monitoring software. The irony is that Alan had little need for a bank apart from its use as a store for his Aim-listed company's income. When it was only four years old, Sabien booked sales in excess of £1 m, benefiting from the fact that at the time, as the economy was struggling and energy prices rising, large companies were eager to cut their fuel bills. It is a situation that looked unlikely to change as this book went to print.

'I don't need debt,' Alan told me. He said most banks that provided loans in his sector were too greedy, so the risk to a growing business like his was too great.

His attitude might surprise the many business owners that are desperate to raise debt finance for working capital. However, it makes perfect sense to those businesses that do not use debt finance.

Russel Griggs, a former chairman of the small business council of the CBI, the UK's main employers' body, insisted to me that the shortage of bank finance had in some ways been a good thing for British enterprise because it has encouraged business owners to look elsewhere for cash – such as invoice financing or equity sales. 'Because there is less money in the banking sector, you have to be more creative,' he said.

Many business owners, however, are continuing to swear off bank debt. This may actually not be a bad thing.

The conclusion

The main message of this chapter is simply that rushing into a bank loan to start a business is not necessarily the best way to get going as an entrepreneur. In fact, conventional term loans are a far less common way of financing a business than most people imagine.

In some countries, credit cards are actually a more popular source of start-up capital.

Bootstrapping, where you build a business using your own resources, is a common way for many ultimately fast-growing businesses to get going. It is also increasingly easy to do, given the low cost of starting a business these days due to falling costs in areas like technology.

It is not that you do not need money to build a great company, but that the way you get it will affect how you operate, which can be crucial in the early stages of a business. You may also fail to create innovations that save money and that may enable your business to grow fast in the future. The disasters of the dotcom boom, when companies failed after burning through millions of dollars in funding, are testament to this.

Timing can be everything in terms of when you get your first major tranche of outside support. It pays to plan well in advance and communicate clearly with the people who can offer you the finance.

Finally, it is worth remembering that raising finance is seldom easy and will usually take a large amount of your time and energy. You therefore need to be prepared for the process.

Chapter Two
Don't innovate, imitate

Entrepreneurs are often mistaken for inventors. They are not.

Inventors are people like Bernhard Grill, Karl-Heinz Brandenburg, Thomas Sporer, Bernd Kurten and Ernst Eberlein, who claimed the patent for MP3 technology that enabled music to be shared on electronic files. However, it was US-based Napster and Swedish start-up Kazaa that used the file sharing technology to create a model for selling music digitally, albeit illegally at first, sparking a round of creative destruction the music industry has never recovered from.

It was then Steve Jobs who convinced the music labels to use his iTunes service to beat the music pirates, and Apple that designed the hardware and software to do this. Jonathan Ive, Apple's design genius, did not invent MP3 players, but he enabled Apple to create a way of listening to music that created a multibillion dollar industry. In the process, Apple created new markets for video and musical content as well as all manner of software programmes developed for its app store.

What this one example shows is how entrepreneurs work. There are some very entrepreneurial inventors, but they are an exception. Most entrepreneurs take another person's technological breakthrough and use their skills in mobilizing resources, publicity, salesmanship and financial management to create a viable business.

Inventors create the technology, but entrepreneurs turn it into something of economic value. It is possible to go a stage further than this, however, because people do not just invent things, such as cars or personal computers, they come up with ideas for new services that people need and ways of providing them.

What this chapter is going to look at is how many successful entrepreneurs have built great businesses by doing what someone else has done, only better. The point of doing this is to show that originality in entrepreneurship is actually an over-rated virtue. Imitation, on the other hand, is not just the sincerest form of flattery. It is one of the shrewdest ways to become a successful rebel entrepreneur.

An imitator in action

Take Lovefilm, the highly successful UK-based start-up that has made renting DVD films and television box sets across Europe as easy as going to the post box or getting online. In January 2011, barely 12 years after it was founded, the company had over 1,500,000 members, each paying a monthly subscription of about £8, a catalogue of over 67,000 film and television programme titles, and over 4 million rentals per month across five countries.

The premise of Lovefilm's business model is simple. Customers pay a monthly fee to receive a number of DVDs or games discs in the post, or the right to download a given quantity over the internet to a TV or tablet device. They can play the games and watch the films as much as they like, and keep them as long as they like, but they will not get a new one until they return the ones they already have. Lovefilm is able to do this because in most western European countries there are two very reliable delivery mechanisms – one very modern (the internet) and the other Victorian (the postal service).

Lovefilm's customers pay a subscription to the company, log onto the website and set up lists of favourite films or games, which are ranked as high, medium or low priority. Lovefilm then picks one or two of these, depending on the customer's price plan, and according to availability in the warehouse, and pops them in the post. Both the old and the new technology work.

Since its creation, Lovefilm has developed its offering to allow customers to bypass the old-economy postal system entirely by streaming video over the internet to get films 'on demand' on their home computer, games console, TV, tablet computer or smartphone.

Pretty neat, huh? Yes, except Lovefilm is completely unoriginal.

The original

Reed Hastings pioneered the idea of DVD rental by post in California back in 1997, allegedly after his shock at receiving a bill for $40 in late fees from Blockbuster, the old-school high-street film rental business. Reed himself had to fine-tune his original idea to make it work. Initially the business model for his company, Netflix, was for customers to pay for each rental individually. In September 1999, he changed this and Netflix started offering monthly subscriptions. The pay-per-rental model was dropped completely a few months later.

It was not for another three years that Lovefilm began trading in Europe. There were advantages to this. By that time, people had been able to see that the idea worked, helping Lovefilm's founders to put their case when they needed backing from investors or to recruit key personnel.

The concept of copying someone else's idea may seem wrong, but it could also be viewed as the most sincere form of validation of what the original innovator–entrepreneur was doing. After all, if you come up with a new kind of product or service and no one else copies you, you have to ask yourself whether it was such a good idea in the first place.

Every action has a legal reaction

There can be copyright issues.

In the case of Netflix, it gained a US patent on its business model in 2003 and sued Blockbuster, an old-school owner of video rental shops that had started operating a very similar service to its own. It was able to do this because Blockbuster was in the United States and it had started its service after Netflix gained its patent. Netflix was too late to stop Lovefilm from doing what it had been doing across the Atlantic in Europe, however.

Some people question whether employing legal protection for a business model is worthwhile in a world where the constant pushing of technological boundaries means that commercial ideas seldom remain the same for long. It could be argued that the best thing any originator can do is to beat its competitors at their own game, since focusing on legal action will take your eye off of the main prize of building a better business.

You can't keep a good idea down

For the pioneer of online DVD rental the problem of plagiarism was more complex because, in Europe at least, the mimicking of its business model was much more widespread than just one company. Several wannabe entrepreneurs had individually thought that they could make the DVD rental-by-post model work in EU countries and so set up rival companies doing the same thing.

In May 2002, Paul Gardner and Graham Bosher launched Online Rentals Limited (trading as DVDsOnTap) in the English new town of Harlow, Essex. ScreenSelect was created in Acton, west London, in September 2003 by William Reeve and Alex Chesterman. In the same month Saul Klein, a South African-born entrepreneur who had spent most of his childhood in the UK, set up Video Island in an office near King's Cross station. Saul had recently returned from the United States, where he had been involved in several start-ups. He had also been involved in the early stages of Skype, the online telephony service developed by a group of software programmers in Tallin, Estonia, and led by the Swedish entrepreneurs Niklas Zennstrom and Janus Friis.

Elsewhere in Europe, Brafilm, a Swedish and Norwegian venture, and Boxman, which operated in Sweden and Denmark, had been created to provide identical DVD rental services in the Nordic region. In the United States, Hollywood Video developed the Movie Value Pass in 2004, which allowed customers to rent up to three movies for a flat monthly fee.

All these businesses were trying to perfect a business model that was, if not identical, very similar to the others.

In the UK, where there were now several brands, a tussle to decide the leader was inevitable. Again this was no bad thing as it forced each start-up to raise its game. The fact that none of these teams were the same was not an issue. In fact, the slight differences in approach and tweaks to each service could act as inspiration to the others to do better, or ape each other.

At some point, however, a consolidation of imitator businesses becomes inevitable.

In October 2003, Online Rentals was bought by Arts Alliance Ventures, a family-owned private equity firm. ScreenSelect led what became a clutch of mergers among the UK players. In December 2003, it acquired In-Movies, then in September 2004 it merged with Video Island, combining ScreenSelect's management and brand with the venture capital backing for Video Island. After a period of intense rivalry, in which both companies grew rapidly, Lovefilm and Screen-Select merged in 2006. The combined business took ScreenSelect's management and technology platform but kept the Lovefilm brand, and moved the headquarters to ScreenSelect's original base in Acton. In all, it took 10 companies to create the final Lovefilm business, each of which had been built on a very similar business model.

The final deal came when Amazon, the online shopping behemoth, bought Lovefilm, making multimillionaires of its investors. This brought the links with Netflix full circle, given that Lovefilm is now part of a US company.

Amazon had seen the potential of the online DVD rental market at first hand with Netflix. Its founder, Jeff Bezos, has a reputation for constantly trying to stretch the Amazon brand into new areas. His approach has often been to try things himself before buying one of the best players in the market – another way of grabbing someone else's good idea. This is exactly what he did with the online DVD rental model. Amazon tried building its own video rental service, based on people downloading titles from its website. This was not as successful as Mr Bezos would have liked, so he bought Lovefilm instead.

Imitator brands have clearly been a benefit for Amazon. In a way they have acted as the research and development function of Amazon, honing the service until it was ready for Amazon to acquire.

First movers do not necessarily have the advantage

One lesson from Netflix and Lovefilm is that a business model is very hard to control in a world of free trade and the free flow of ideas, even with patent protection.

Another lesson from this story is that the first to market is never guaranteed first place. That prize goes to the entrepreneur who can out-execute his or her rivals.

Sometimes it can be the innovators' own fault that they fall behind. In 2011, while Lovefilm expanded across Europe and positioned itself to launch in the United States, Netflix stumbled. In a move presumably meant to encourage people to move towards the more advanced and cost-effective downloading service, Reed Hastings announced in July of that year that Netflix customers who received films in the post would have to pay $16 a month for the service rather than $10 a month. This 60 per cent hike in prices sparked a revolt and Netflix customers began cancelling their subscriptions immediately.

Just a few weeks after the price increase was announced Netflix had lost a million subscribers, it was claimed. The company's share price also dropped, tumbling by 15 per cent when the decline in subscriber numbers was revealed.

An announcement that the company was going to split its video-by-post operation from its downloading service was quickly reversed.

The battle of the online DVD rental companies is not yet over, and Netflix could indeed prove the victor. The companies are going head-to-head in Europe after Netflix launched in the UK market.

However, these kinds of stories, in which smart business ideas are adopted by imitators, are played out in all sorts of markets. Imitation is also a lot older than the internet sector. It happens in airlines (where Ryanair apes the budget airline model pioneered by Southwest Airlines), banking (Metro Bank in the UK is a direct copy of Commerce Bank in the United States) and retail (in which the UK's Asda openly borrowed from the stack 'em high, sell 'em cheap model perfected by Walmart in the United States during the 1990s). Some of these copycat businesses are made to create a global challenger brand, others with the blessing (and even the financial backing) of the original business founders.

The fact that there are very few truly original business ideas, how-ever, does not seem to be a problem. There are plenty of ways to take an existing idea and tweak it to make it a much bigger proposition.

Copying is as old as the hills

The fact is that there is very little in the world that is new anymore. Even things we think are relatively recent may not be as earth-shatteringly modern as we think. Back in 1919, in his book *The Economic Consequences of the Peace*, the British economist John Maynard Keynes waxed lyrical about a new business model created by the invention of a wonderful medium of communication called the telephone. 'The inhabitant of London could order by telephone, sipping his morning tea in bed, the various products of the whole earth, in such quantity as he might see fit, and reasonably expect their early delivery upon his doorstep,' he wrote.

Eighty years later, this same business model (albeit one using the world wide web rather than analogue telephone systems) was being praised by a new generation of economists talking up the ideas of online retailers like Amazon.com, or internet grocery delivery services like Ocado in the UK.

Not that echoing a tried and tested idea is a guarantee of success. Many of the dotcom retail businesses that popped up in the 1990s, with their posturing about new economics and hyper-efficient delivery mechanisms, proved to be duds. One of the greatest disasters was Boo.com, the European online fashion retailer launched in 1999, which burnt through $135 m of venture capital money in 18 months before declaring itself bankrupt in May 2000.

Another failure was Webvan, a Californian online grocery delivery business started by one of the co-founders of the Borders bookshop chain, which filed for bankruptcy protection just 18 months after its shares were listed on the public stock market. This was not necessarily because the idea of online grocery shopping was bad. Tesco, the successful real-world retailer, made online grocery shopping profitable in the UK by using the tried and tested technique of only delivering from its existing stores.

Webvan had taken a different approach, building its own distribution centres and delivering from them, largely because it did not have the advantage of starting with a large chain of supermarket buildings, like Tesco. However, the problem for Webvan was fundamentally one of execution. The company tried to grow quickly without the customer demand to support it. It was not that Webvan customers did not like the service – parents with young children in particular found the option of avoiding the trip out for a weekly food shop a boon – it was just that there were not enough of them.

Webvan was not alone in making this mistake. In 1999, when the company completed its initial public offering, most internet analysts just felt dotcom businesses would soak up demand because of their superior services. Although that demand has since arrived, it took a lot longer to come than most at the time expected.

The model for Ocado has many similarities with the approach taken by Webvan, except that it is still in business. A large part of this is down to execution. Although Ocado has also had to follow a long road before reaching profitability, and still faces many tests ahead in what is now a highly competitive online grocery market in its native UK market, it differed in its approach from Webvan in several ways. One of these was its pace of growth. Ocado started on a relatively small scale with a geographic area it knew would give it some critical mass. It then built demand for its service before expanding further.

Webvan had rushed to expand and severely overstretched itself. At the time it closed, it delivered groceries in Chicago, Los Angeles, Orange County, California, Portland, Oregon, San Diego, San Francisco and Seattle. Ocado, in comparison, grew its facilities at a snail's pace, taking eight years to open its second distribution centre. But this was good because it was in step with demand.

Ocado also took advantage of a relationship with an existing bricks-and-mortar retailer, the upmarket supermarket group Waitrose, which gave it both products that people trusted and were willing to pay a premium for, and the backing of an established brand. Although Waitrose has now set up its own online grocery delivery service, previously it had a strong incentive to help make Ocado work.

Smart imitators don't just learn from their own mistakes, they learn from those of others.

Imitation of business models is probably most obvious in the internet sector. This might be due to the industry being so young and easy to access. If someone has a good idea, like connecting with old friends online or selling shirts, it is highly likely that some-one else on the planet has already been thinking about it and so will do something similar. Also, in the virtual world, where everyone and everything is only a shrewd Google search away, if someone spots something that works as a business, it is relatively cheap and easy for others to see it and set up something similar.

The internet has spawned an array of copycat business models, largely because it is so young and so there is so much that is still possible using online networks and has not been tried yet.

We may all now think of Amazon as the only online book retailer on the planet (in fact, it is now the largest department store on the planet), but there were plenty of others that did the same thing before it. Many of them failed, however, to get the execution right. Once Amazon did start to pull ahead, it also acted fast to consolidate its lead, buying up other national players that were creating similar businesses. In the process it was able to improve its own technology and create a global footprint that made the business stronger.

Imitators can therefore be good news for the originator too. In late 1996, for instance, Simon Murdoch launched Bookpages, an online bookseller for the UK. In April 1998, Amazon decided it liked Bookpages so much it bought the company, making Simon a multi-millionaire. In the October of that year, it relaunched the business as Amazon.co.uk, and appointed Simon as its European vice-president. He went on to help set up Amazon's German and French operations. Bookpages had been doing what Amazon had done, but it had done it slightly differently, using different technology. However, this was research and development that Amazon could use, so the copying served both parties well.

For Simon Murdoch, Bookpages was just the start of his journey in entrepreneurship. Since the Amazon deal, he has used his wealth to help other technology ventures get off the ground in Europe. As a former chairman of Video Island, he also has a link with Lovefilm – the technology industry might be global but it sometimes feels like a small cabal of friends.

Another service made possible by the internet is price comparison websites. Again this is a business model open to multiple repetitions, creating millions of pounds in value even for the also-rans. In the UK, Moneysupermarket.com and Comparethemarket.com quickly established themselves as market leaders in the sector. However, this did not stop John Paleomylites, a technology entrepreneur who had already built and sold one business, from using the business model to enter the market himself with his company Beatthatquote.com.

I first met John during the dotcom boom years of the 1990s when he was running his first IT start-up, a London-based security software business called JCP that he later sold to Sun Microsystems of the United States. His timing on that deal had been perfect since just a few weeks after the contracts were signed, the dotcom bubble burst, sending share prices of technology stocks plummeting.

By the time I reconnected with John in 2006, he had become a proponent of the bootstrapping model we have already looked at in Chapter 1 of this book. The contrast between his first and second venture in this regard was stark. JCP required two rounds of funding to get to the size it did, and ended up raising a shade below £4m. Beatthatquote.com on the other hand was started on a credit card with a credit facility from John's bank, HSBC. Although John was not short of cash personally by this point, he showed a steely determination to keep the cost of his second venture to a minimum. One of the ways he did this was to launch Beatthatquote.com from his living room table, taking on serviced office space only as the enterprise grew.

John was not only trying to learn from someone else's business model to build his new company, he was learning from his own experience with his first business. He also made sure he researched his new venture well, spending 18 months studying the market before launching Beatthatquote.com. This was a luxury he could afford in part because he had wealth of his own from his first business. But it was time well spent because he was able to see exactly how others operated before starting himself, and so try to avoid their mistakes.

'You either raise a significant amount of money that you can use to fund yourself while you refine your business model, or you ensure that the model is right,' he told me. Although, or perhaps because, John was taking on a proven business model, the returns from Beatthatquote.com were impressive. In its first year of trading, Beatthatquote.com made a profit of £99,000 on a £1.4m turnover. In the following 12 months this rose to a £4m profit on revenues of £12m.

This made Beatthatquote.com one of the fastest growing companies in the UK at that time.

It is all about execution

We have already seen the power of execution in turning an imitator model into a success.

In the case of Beatthatquote.com, John's idea was to use his IT experience to give his business more efficient systems for connecting borrowers with lenders – the key to higher margins and bigger profits. He had some initial success in this area.

After the first year of trading, Beatthatquote.com employed one-twentieth of the people working at Moneysupermarket.com, its biggest rival, but Beatthatquote.com's revenues were less than 10 times as large.

He also learnt from mistakes he felt he had made in his first venture. One of these was in the area of staff. In JCP, John felt he had tried to run things his way for too long at the beginning. Therefore, when it came to Beatthatquote.com he made sure he put good people into key positions when setting up the business, then delegated a lot of responsibility to them. Pulling in the talent was made easier both because John could boast a successful track record and because several of the people he has brought on board at Beatthatquote.com were colleagues from JCP.

The story of Beatthatquote.com did not end in the company overtaking those it was imitating, but it was a result that was in some ways just as good for the founder – the company got bought. In March 2011, Google snapped it up for £37.7 m.

Being acquired is an often under-rated mark of success. It might not allow a founder to achieve world domination, but it enables shareholders to realize a return on their investment and can liberate the owner to go and do it again with another business that may be even bigger and better. It can also, as the Amazon–Bookpages deal did, enhance the larger company.

The fact that large companies do often acquire companies that do what either they or their competitors are doing is in some ways another argument for imitating rather than innovating as a founder. It gives you another method of exiting your business if you choose.

Attack of the clones

Not that those who consider themselves the innovators can be expected to see it that way. In the United States, successful web firms that have had their businesses copied by foreign entrepreneurs refer disdainfully to their alien rivals as 'clones'. The fact that the word also conjures images of the evil empire in the *Star Wars* series is no coincidence.

One example of a company that has been attacked by the clones is Airbnb, a US-based online marketplace that helps people rent rooms, which has had run-ins with 9flats, a Berlin-based copy. It is easy to sympathize with Airbnb, not least because 9flats adapted its business model to match changes Airbnb has made to its service.

Three brothers in Germany, Alexander, Oliver and Marc Samwer, have made a career of launching clone businesses based on ideas first formed in Silicon Valley. Their first success was in 1999 with Alando, an online auction house, which they later sold to eBay for $50 m. They have since created cember.net, an online business network, sold to Xing for $6.4 m, and CityDeal, a copy of discount vouchers business Groupon, sold to the US-based company for $126 m.

What probably riles the US-based originals most is that they often end up having to buy the companies that have copied them. However, it could be argued that the clones are doing the US-based companies they have copied a favour by creating an instant foothold in foreign markets. Without CityDeal, Groupon would have had to have built its own market share in Germany, the cost of which could have been enormous.

There is also something of a double standard at play here since successful US-based start-ups are often followed by a number of home-grown companies chasing exactly the same opportunity. When this happens, the rivals are not derided as clones, but merely described as competitors in the US media.

Imitation can be the salvation of a company

A company may not start out copying another person's business model. But it may just be its salvation to imitate another's ideas at a later stage.

It could be said this was the case for what the supermarket Asda did when it took on Walmart's way of working. Like many of the Samwer brothers' ventures, Asda, the UK's second largest supermarket chain, ended up being bought by the company it was aping. This is in part because Walmart wanted to expand into Europe but also because, with near-identical business cultures, the two businesses were very easy to assimilate. For the last few years before its sale, Asda's then chief executive Archie Norman had been actively copying the things that made Walmart such a success, such as focusing on being the lowest-price food retailer in the market.

In many ways this copying of the Walmart model came late in the day to Asda, whose roots can be traced back to the early twentieth century and a family of butchers in West Yorkshire called the Asquiths. The original Asda business, formed through a merger of the Asquith's operations with other Yorkshire food retailers, actually shared some similarities with the aspirations of Walmart in that it was known for offering good value for money and price competitiveness. It had grown to a national chain by the 1980s, but then got into trouble, partly because it had got away from its original value proposition.

It was this founding principle of Asda that provided a common link with Walmart when Mr Norman took over and turned the business around. Aping Walmart more completely must have seemed a logical progression at the time.

Even for those inspired enough to come up with a business model that seems genuinely unique there will come a day when someone looks to copy the idea. After all, if nobody wants to copy your business idea you have to ask whether it was such a good idea in the first place.

Rupert Merson, adjunct associate professor of entrepreneurship at London Business School, describes the process of being copied almost as a rite of passage for young businesses. 'I hear of lots of companies saying that they have no competition, when what they mean is they haven't been noticed yet,' he told me. Companies that have their product, service or business model copied should perhaps cheer because it is proof they have something worth copying.

It is what you do once your business model has been copied that often makes the difference. If a large multinational starts to sell the same product as you, it may be the chance to do a deal with it, either through a joint venture or perhaps even a trade sale. After all, if you cannot beat them, why not join them, as Asda did with Walmart?

Another option is to seek out a rival of the company you have copied to team up with. This can be seen in the story of Innocent Drinks, which in 1998 brought what was then a very pioneering idea to the UK in the form of smoothies. The business was started by three Cambridge graduates, who knew each other from their time studying at St John's College: Richard Reed, Adam Balon and Jon Wright.

From the start, they built an image based on maverick behaviour and fun. Legend has it that the company was formed after the trio tried selling their healthy drinks at a music festival in London. People were asked to put their empty bottles in bins marked either 'yes' or 'no' to register whether they thought the three should quit their jobs to make smoothies. At the end of the festival the 'yes' bin was full, with only three cups in the 'no' bin, so the friends went to their work the next day and resigned.

Other quirky factors about Innocent were the ways they worked. The company's London headquarters was named Fruit Towers and their delivery vans were covered from bonnet to boot in astroturf. The founders also set up a charitable foundation, pledging to give 10 per cent of profits to charity each year.

Their first big business break came when Maurice Pinto, a wealthy American businessman, decided to invest £250,000 in the fledgling operation.

Innocent has been the only company to grow so fast and consistently in the UK in recent years that it has appeared in the *Sunday Times* newspaper's Fast Track 100 for five consecutive years.

This was an original business model that worked, so it was not long before someone came along to copy it. Unlike the examples given already in this chapter, however, the new entrant was a long-established company many, many times the size of Innocent. It was PepsiCo that in 2008, 10 years after Innocent had started, decided to launch into the smoothie market in the UK, using its fresh fruit juice brand Tropicana.

In the months after Tropicana Smoothies came onto the market, Innocent reported a 5 per cent drop in sales and for the first time in its history had to get rid of some of its staff. On 6 April 2009, the company announced its agreement to sell a small stake, between 10 and 20 per cent, in its operations to the Coca-Cola Company for £30 m. The news did not please Innocent's customers, who bombarded the company website with complaints. This did not stop Innocent going further and in April 2010 it was announced that Coca-Cola had increased its stake to 58 per cent for an investment of about £65 m.

What did make sense about the deal was the fact that Coca-Cola was the arch rival of PepsiCo.

Whether it was Innocent that sought out Coca-Cola after PepsiCo muscled in on its market, or it was Coca-Cola that saw the opportunity, Innocent's founders have never said. Either way, however, the arrival of a copycat product created an opportunity.

One of the refreshing aspects of entrepreneurship is it is not limited to one particular place. Those in the start-up community talk about an 'ecosystem', which equates to the necessary intellectual capital, economic freedoms and finance needed to support new ventures.

However, there are many places around the world where these raw ingredients can be found. We have talked a lot in this chapter about digital business models, perhaps because these are among the most simple to transfer across borders. Different countries and cities have recently got into a contest to see who can claim that they are the next Silicon Valley, as if this were the secret to becoming the most entrepreneurial place on the planet. Singapore, Bangalore, Berlin, Cambridge, New York and London have all made this comparison, usually with the encouragement of the city governments.

This kind of imitation may not be helpful, however, since it is very difficult for an entire region to replicate another's recipe for success. The smarter approach for city or national governments would be to look at comparative advantages, such as the strengths in different industry sectors, which may in fact have more potential than just microprocessors, the basis of Silicon Valley's success.

The leading cluster of the future is in fact more likely to be built around something other than silicon because computing power is now so much more pervasive and cheap (since Moore's Law has proved to be true). Just as previous clusters, like the shipbuilding talent of Glasgow or the banking expertise of medieval Florence, have waxed and waned, so the pervasiveness of internet technology is likely to make a cluster based purely on IT a weaker proposition in 20 years' time. Even in the market for internet-based services, we are seeing business models originate on the other side of the globe from California.

The internet's cut-price fashion revolution started, perhaps unsurprisingly, in Milan, where the founders of Yoox.com persuaded big Italian brands to sell end-of-season products online. The idea was simple: take the real-world success of 'flash' sales, where designer labels offload excess stock at deep discounts, usually in disused industrial buildings, and put them on in the virtual world, where the process can be done on a much larger scale through people just logging onto the website.

Yoox.com, which kept people up to date with offers via e-mail, was founded in 2000. It took less than a year for the idea to be copied and launched as Vente-Privée in Paris, another of Europe's fashion capitals, by Jacques-Antoine Granjon.

Once again the first mover did not have the advantage. This was partly because the follower was led by a sharp-minded founder.

Jacques-Antoine was a born businessman from a family of entrepreneurs, and a graduate of the prestigious European Business School. He also had a long history in the fashion discount sector from the pre-web days, when it was all about outlet stores and twice-yearly stock sales. In 1985, he founded overstock distributor Cofotex with his student friend Julien Sorbac. Eleven years later, he bought and renovated the former print works of national French newspaper *Le Monde* in La Plaine Saint-Denis, just outside of Paris. This became the headquarters for Vente-Privée.

In January 2001, the website vente-privee.com began trading. Although Yoox had begun several months previously, Vente-Privée quickly became the market leader in France and across continental Europe. The company set itself up as a business 'with a conscience', offering responsible growth, training, employability and social responsibility. It grew rapidly. By 2010, Vente-Privée was employing more than 1,350 people. Its sales of €680 m were a third higher than a year earlier.

Such an incredibly successful idea was never going to be ignored for long by other entrepreneurs, especially those in the technology heartland of the United States. Across the Atlantic, a number of flash-sale websites started springing up, such as Rue La La, One Kings Lane, Hautelook and Beyond the Rack.

Although Silicon Valley tried to get a slice of this market, the most successful attempts at the business model came from elsewhere. In this case New York. Ideeli and Gilt Groupe opened within a couple of months of each other in 2007 in Manhattan, which, like Vente-Privée's home town Paris, was a prime market for luxury clothing.

Again, however, it was not the first mover that gained the advantage. Gilt came later to the market than even its peers in New York, but managed to eclipse them all. Growth at Gilt has been exponential. As I write this, the company has just announced plans to double its revenue to $1 bn in 12 months.

So what is it that makes one company so much more successful than others with near-identical business models? The degree of experience of the founders certainly seems to play a part. Just as Vente-Privée benefited from being created by someone who understood the outlet sale model, Gilt has been helped by its founder, Kevin Ryan, having a good grasp of the online world.

Kevin was already an experienced entrepreneur. I first met him in New York in the early noughties when he was running DoubleClick, an online advertising business that he managed to bring back from a near-death experience following the bursting of the dotcom bubble. We will return to this concept of learning from failure in a later chapter. However, suffice it to say that Kevin's pain clearly taught him some valuable lessons in making a business idea work whatever the market or the concept. Experience can therefore play a part in making a business idea a success. But what really sets the start-up success stories apart from the also-rans is execution.

This is where Gilt has been able to set itself apart from its competition, first in the United States and then across the world. One of the innovations of Gilt during its early days was to launch a referral system, where the company paid customers $25 for every other person they could get to sign up. Nowadays such systems have been used by all sorts of online services and to an extent have lost their appeal. But Gilt was among the first and as such created a lot of excitement in Manhattan. Fashion bloggers would provide links through their websites to claim their Gilt rewards. 'We had people who made literally thousands of dollars referring our service to their friends,' Rob Denning, one of Gilt's early employees, explained to me. Although Gilt was paying a lot through the referral system, this more than paid for itself in new business.

The cost of customer acquisition is by far the largest expense for any online start-up. The referral system meant that Gilt was adding people for a quarter of the price its rivals were paying, according to Rob.

The referral system is no longer a source of competitive advantage. It was itself widely copied by online businesses as a way to attract new customers, and as such lost a lot of the original appeal among consumers that made it such an attractive strategy in the first place. It also only tended to work as a strategy in certain markets. When Gilt launched in Japan, it tried the referral system again, but this time with much less impressive results. The problem, it transpired, was that the Japanese were too concerned about losing face if their friend did not like the Gilt experience.

Superior execution is not always due to planning. It can sometimes be pure good luck. Gilt had the good fortune to launch in a recession when the major fashion labels were more desperate than usual to offload their unsold stock. As a result, it was able to offer itself as a solution to the industry's problem.

This is not to take away from the genius of Kevin. He recognized early on in Gilt's evolution that the fashion industry might not get that excited about a 50-something former technology-industry founder. Indeed he was having trouble convincing the luxury fashion labels he was the kind of person they could trust to take care of their brands. So he did something to give them confidence in his brand.

Kevin's original team included eBay executive Alexis Maybank, and Alexandra Wilkis Wilson, merchandizing executive for Louis Vuitton and Bulgari. They had credibility with the fashion label heads, so Kevin made them the public face of the company. The story of Alexis and Alexandra as the founders of Gilt was not just a good way to get the merchandise suppliers on board. The success of a couple of female entrepreneurs provided an angle for the media to cover the Gilt story at an early stage in its development, further helping the brand get established.

Timing is everything

Just at the key moment, when Gilt needed to switch its story from that of a plucky start-up to the one about its preparations for an IPO, Kevin came back to the fore, taking over the role of chief executive.

It takes a lot of humility, it seems, to be a successful rebel entrepreneur.

Kevin's killer execution was also about his choice of location for the business. Having New York as a home market meant that Gilt's core early audience not only understood the importance of fashion but had large amounts of money to spend on it. 'Being in New York, you have great brands, better customers and better marketing,' Kevin told me, when I asked how Gilt was able to become such a success in such a short period of time. The typical Gilt customer is in her early thirties, lives in Manhattan and earns between $100,000 and $120,000 a year, according to Kevin.

When we met late in London in 2011, he had a whole lot more numbers at his finger tips. Understanding the numbers of course is another key to successful executors of business models. Kevin was able to be quite specific about his most profitable customers. The top 65, for instance, spend over $100,000 a year with Gilt (indeed, the largest single spender purchased $500,000 of clothing from Gilt in a year). Another 10,000 to 20,000 people spend $10,000 annually with the business.

Knowledge is power and customers are the lifeblood of any business. If you have richer, more engaged customers, as arguably Gilt had in even greater numbers than its French or Italian counterparts, then you have a better chance of expanding faster. However, that is not enough.

In Gilt's case, market domination is in large part due to its success in expanding the concept beyond its core audience of rich metropolitan New York women. It has the advantage of all US-based start-ups in that it has an enormous domestic market. Although Gilt does not have many rural customers, there are plenty of target shoppers in the large American cities, such as Chicago, Miami and San Francisco.

However, Gilt has not just expanded geographically. It has looked for new applications of the flash-sale concept in other retail sectors. The company may have started, like all its contemporaries, in female fashions but it has gone after different demographics, opening a men's outlet store and selling items other than clothes, such as home wares and travel. As a result, Gilt is now a source for all sorts of hard-to-find luxury goods, from vintage guitars to Rolex watches, and even classic cars.

'I think we have most of the large categories that we want to be in,' Kevin told me. However, I got the feeling that he was open to further expansion if his staff could prove it would work. It is that sort of testing that enables rebel entrepreneurs to gain the necessary edge and keep one step ahead of their competitors.

Bridal wear is something Gilt has yet to create a category for, but Kevin admitted to me when I saw him that they had experimented by offering a packaged deal for the special day, called 'Wedding in a box'. It took just 11 minutes for the $30,000 service to be snapped up by someone and 34 others were put on a waiting list. It is experimentation like this that has enabled Kevin's team to spot interesting new avenues for the business.

This kind of diversification is a major shift away from the original business model for flash sales of clothing but can be seen as a source of strength as Gilt seeks world domination. It offers lessons for others that it is never enough to just copy another entrepreneur's plan. You have to improve upon it.

For example, a quarter of Gilt's customers are men. Spreading the demographic is at least part of the reason why Gilt has been able to expand faster than its peers.

When you ask Kevin about why Gilt has performed better than its rivals, he agrees that it is not so much a matter of innovation but of execution. 'We are broadly the same business [as all these other companies] but we have better people,' he told me.

You do not have to settle for second best

It is important for those that out-execute on other people's business models not to rest on their laurels once they have got ahead. After all, as Netflix found to its cost, it is easy to mess up and lose millions of customers. In an increasingly competitive market like the one for flash sales, you cannot afford such errors.

If you do continue to execute well and innovate with your model, you can extend your lead.

One of the advantages of an internet-based model is that you can quickly get momentum once you have made an idea work, and Kevin has lots of experience of doing this with his other internet ventures over the years. 'Every example you can think of in the internet, there is one player who pulls ahead,' he said. 'People don't write about the guy who is a distant second.'

Like the battle between Lovefilm and Netflix, however, the tussle between Gilt and Vente-Privée is not yet over. While Gilt grabs headlines in the United States, Vente-Privée has been building a powerful base in Europe. The two companies have now reached a stage where they are expanding into each other's home territories.

Gilt's approach has been to take advantage of the fact that Europe, while technically a single market, is really many divided geographies. As a result it launched its European entry in London rather than Paris, which it seems happy to leave to its more established rival. Vente-Privée has to convince the American consumers that its offering is superior. Its problem may be the perception among Americans that it is an outsider. It formed a partnership with American Express in part to help overcome this barrier. If it can do so, Vente-Privée may have the advantage over Gilt, in that the United States is a single market that it can move across more quickly than Gilt can in the EU.

The problem for Vente-Privée is that it has yet to diversify in the way Gilt has done. There are even rumours that Vente-Privée could be an acquisition target for a more generalist online retailer like Amazon.

For Gilt, success has created its own army of imitators. These companies are not trying to recreate the whole of Gilt, but rather to copy the specific categories for flash sales it has created, such as travel. Gilt appears to be taking an enlightened approach to such start-ups, reasoning that new entrants in the market can only raise awareness of the service. Once new customers have entered the market through rival businesses, it is then up to Gilt to attract them to its services.

Its advantage will be that it can offer a lot more than just one category. It is up to Gilt to make the most of this.

The conclusion

All this reinforces what this chapter is all about.

Firstly, entrepreneurs are not inventors. The most successful ones may also not be the innovators who come up with the new business models.

However, in order to be a successful entrepreneur you do need to be able to out-execute everyone else in your market. This means that you need to be able to spot the opportunities to improve on what you started with, even if it was someone else's idea.

Copying can be good for both the innovator and the imitator. It can increase the size of a market, thus increasing the prize for the eventual market champion.

Imitators that start up in another part of the world may also become an acquisition target for the innovator company, saving it the cost of working out how to make its concept work in another geography.

Imitation is not just the sincerest form of flattery, it is a form of validation for the innovator's idea. If you do not have any imitators, you may have to ask yourself whether your business idea is that good.

Imitation is a two-way process. If you do have imitators, their ideas can help you hone your model and improve it.

Aping another model can be useful even if you do not become the largest player in the market, because you may well become an acquisition target for one of your competitors. As a result, you have a perfectly acceptable exit strategy.

Finally, the key to any successful business is good execution. That is far more important than having the idea for a certain business model.

Chapter Three
Don't be a hero

One of the main reasons people give up seemingly safe jobs and secure careers to risk what most of their friends, family and former colleagues will tell them is the much more precarious future of a start-up business is the wonderful, beguiling charisma of a founder.

An entrepreneur's can-do attitude can be infectious, which also happens to be useful if you are going to ask a group of people to risk everything to come and work for you. Self-belief is also often the vital ingredient needed to make a success of something that many others have probably already claimed cannot be done. This explains why some of the world's best-known entrepreneurs also display something of a messianic quality. While the world around them seems full of trouble and upset, these leaders exude hope and a feeling that anything is possible if only they have the people and resources to do it.

A prime example of this is Sir Richard Branson, one of the best-known faces of entrepreneurship in the world. Like that other well-known British brand, Marmite, Sir Richard tends to divide public opinion sharply – you either love him or you hate him. There has been some argument over the degree of success achieved by the individual businesses within his Virgin empire, and there have been notable failures such as Virgin Cola and the cosmetics brand Vie. But few can deny that Sir Richard has also brought about enormous change through his different ventures – a classic rebel entrepreneur.

Publicity has always been his strength. This is the man who signed punk band The Sex Pistols to his fledgling Virgin Records label in the 1970s, achieving considerable notoriety in the process.

He broke the rules again in 1984 with the creation of Virgin Atlantic against the backdrop of one of the worst periods for the airline industry – just two years after Freddie Laker's no-frills airline had gone bust and while the industry was being pushed into deregulation in the UK. It has been for many years one of Sir Richard's most profitable ventures, and its routes criss-cross the planet, flying from New Delhi to London to Cape Town to Los Angeles.

The Virgin brand reaches just as far with other services, from mobile phones to credit cards. He promises one day to take people into space through his Virgin Galactic business.

How has Sir Richard – one man – been able to achieve so much? The truth is that he has not. While his personality has inspired many both inside and outside his companies, it is his ability to find good people to run his empire, then leave them to get on with it, that has been the secret of his success.

This is the point of this chapter. Heroes are all very well in business, but the most consistently successful entrepreneurs are those that do exactly what Sir Richard has done and allow other people, better suited to the role than themselves, to run the show.

I was fortunate enough to be able to interview Sir Richard for the *Financial Times* in 2011, the two of us sharing the back of a Lexus and talking as he travelled between venues in London's West End following the launch of his latest book, *Screw Business As Usual*. It allowed me to see the Branson magic first hand.

Sir Richard has an uncanny ability to set people at ease and make them feel important. We had met at New Zealand House near Piccadilly Circus, where he had gathered other members of the press with some of the people mentioned in his book. Once we had been introduced, we needed to get the lift down to the basement to collect the car where I would be able to get Sir Richard's undivided attention for the interview. As we waited in the corridor, a complete stranger came up and started propositioning Sir Richard with his new business idea. He asked if Sir Richard would like to be involved. Instead of rushing away, Sir Richard listened carefully, smiled and told the man what a great idea he had. Rather than letting him down, he said the man should talk to his assistant.

When we got in the lift, this being New Zealand House, a group of Kiwi women squeezed in with us. They had never met Sir Richard before but they immediately felt comfortable enough to open a conversation with him, asking whether he had flown to New Zealand to see any of the recent rugby world cup first hand. He had, of course, and remarked how much he had enjoyed meeting the captain of the All Blacks. It was as if Sir Richard was in the lift catching up with some old friends.

This sunny exchange was all the more remarkable because he was probably exhausted. Later he would fly out to Los Angeles for Virgin's annual Rock the Kasbah charity party on Sunset Boulevard. The following morning he would be back on another flight to his Caribbean retreat, Necker Island.

However, as I travelled with him around London he always acted as if everyone he was talking to at that moment was the most interesting person he had met. Call it British public schoolboy charm, but it was beguiling to watch.

A lot of entrepreneurs have this charismatic hold. What sets the good ones apart from the rest is their ability to let others take control. 'If I have one skill, it is definitely the art of delegation,' he explained. 'And the art of spotting talent.' The man who took on British Airways, which was at the time 'the world's favourite airline' for the volume of business it was doing, and at least proved a match for it; the man who rescued the once-bankrupt bank Northern Rock with his lender Virgin Money; and the man who plans one day to take people on flights into space through his company Virgin Galactic, claims that his greatest skill is to let other people do the work.

The problem of letting go

It must be said first of all that what we are not talking about here is the inability to work hard. Most entrepreneurs seem to relish the opportunity to start early and work late, throwing themselves into the tasks of the day, focusing on what needs to be done and giving, as improbable as it sounds, 100 per cent. In the early days it is vital to muck in, not least because you may well be the only employee for a while. The problems occur as the company starts to grow. At first it is a relief to find someone else to do some of your work, but then anxieties creep in about whether someone is doing the job well and whether you are doing enough yourself.

The hero, so important in the early days, cannot help becoming a meddler, unable to let others take charge of the key decisions and actions needed to enable the business to grow.

Most people find good leadership hard

The words 'hero' and 'meddler' are not mine but those of Cranfield School of Management, created for BGP, the leadership training programme I have talked about in Chapter 1.

Heroes are defined as those who believe they can perform most jobs in the business better than anyone else. They tend to be the people who like to take charge of client relationships, spend lots of their time managing day-to-day operations, and relish the prospect of jumping in and fixing things when problems occur.

Those who have been running the BGP course for a while, such as project director David Molian, claim that heroes and meddlers are a common occurrence. He told me that most of the entrepreneurs he has dealt with through BGP over the years have had character traits that can act against their organization's expansion. He described heroes and meddlers as 'dangerous' to a growing business because they create a bottleneck, preventing others from flourishing. He also claimed that almost two-thirds of senior staff in small businesses leave within two years of their appointment, usually because their relationship with a heroic or meddling owner-manager gets too frustrating.

Being a hero is not just bad for your company and the talented people you have employed. It is bad for you. Trying to remain in day-to-day control while the business outgrows your talents is one of the main reasons why owner-managers get burnt out or just bored. This in turn can lead to people selling their businesses unnecessarily early in their life, a decision they often later regret, according to David. 'You shouldn't confuse getting bored with your job with getting bored with your business,' he told me.

Size is everything

The transformation of a hard-working, highly competent entre-preneur into a hero or a meddler tends to start when a business reaches a certain size. There is some debate about the exact point, but the approximate moment is when your headcount passes the 50-person mark. This is when a business needs processes rather than personalities to drive it forward. It is often also when a founder often needs to make way for an outside chief executive.

Brian Chernett, himself an experienced entrepreneur, explained the process to me. Brian's main focus for 14 of the last 16 years has been the Academy for Chief Executives, a mentoring and networking group, through which he and other experienced founders coached dozens of senior business figures.

He is now taking the ultimate back seat, having sold the business in 2010. But the Academy continues its vital work, nurturing and guiding other British business leaders. Brian can therefore speak from both personal and professional experience when he says that there comes a time for everyone to step back from the business they created.

One of the main reasons why a founder needs to remove him- or herself from the day-to-day functioning of a business is hubris, Brian explained. The problem is that most successful founders end up believing that the only way to run their company is the way that they have done it. 'A good founder is somebody who can see that they haven't got all the skills and experience needed to develop a business,' he told me.

Brian is widely acknowledged as a wise man when it comes to the art of entrepreneurship, but even he admits it is not easy to put the theory of good leadership into practice. 'It takes a lot of courage to do this,' he admitted when I probed him about the need to step back from your business at a certain point. 'I should have done it five years ago.'

Take a tip from the good parenting guide

Of course, no one becomes a hero or meddler because they want to be one. This is why it is so difficult to avoid it.

Founding a business is often likened to the process of becoming a parent. Both involve creating something and nurturing it into maturity. The similarity is obvious in the language founders often use for their business, describing it as their 'baby' or 'child'. The analogy can be useful to explain the dangers of heroics and meddling.

Close supervision of a business, just as for a child, is vital in the early days. But, as any parent knows, babies and children turn into teenagers, then young adults. The secret to good parenting is to let your offspring stand on their own two feet. If you do not step back and let your child develop in his or her own way, you may actually be limiting what that person can do. In the case of human nurturing, it may be that your child needs the guidance of others more than yours as he or she grows up – it might be a particular teacher at their school, a youth group leader or a friend.

When it comes to nurturing business, it may be that the original founders need to hand their enterprise on to outsiders in the form of a new chief executive and board of directors. As any loving parent will tell you, letting go of the one you love is never easy. But it is necessary for the greater good. The same is true for an entrepreneur and his or her business.

One of those who has managed the process of stepping back from day-to-day operations is Nick Jenkins, founder and now executive chairman of online greetings card company, Moonpig. This is another classic example of a disruptive business model of the digital age, using the world wide web not just to cut out the middle man in an everyday transaction (in this case selling greetings cards), but to make an everyday task better.

Buying your Moonpig card online saves the hassle of having to traipse to the high street to leaf through the more limited selection at a card shop. However, what is really clever about selling cards online is the ability for users to personalize their cards, uploading pictures from their computer or smartphone and rewriting the message. In doing so, Moonpig not only makes customers happier by bringing out their inner card designer but makes them part of the production process, thus reducing the need for extra staff to come up with new card designs. In this way, Nick Jenkins has not only handed over power from himself to his staff, but he has even handed it on to his customers.

I first met Nick at his company's headquarters in the stereotypical web business venue, a former warehouse building, tucked behind the Tate Modern art museum in central London. The creative value of customers is celebrated in the office, with some of their best designs being projected onto a large screen in the middle of the office, framed to make it look like a constantly changing picture, and no doubt to remind staff exactly why they are working there.

Although it is therefore clear that customers are doing some of the work, Moonpig still needs to employ its own designers to come up with card templates. It also needs programmers to ensure the technology keeps up with new developments such as the ability to upload pictures from smartphones, as well as all the back office functions. The office space is therefore relaxed and fun. It also remains a company with the founder's name stamped on it – Moonpig was Mr Jenkins's nickname at boarding school.

Web businesses like Moonpig have the advantage of being able to grow fast with little additional headcount and can command much larger margins than their offline equivalents. In 2008, for instance, pre-tax profits more than doubled to £6.7m ($11m, €7.4m) on a turnover of almost £21m. Unlike many other internet start-ups, however, Moonpig is also a manufacturing operation, using Guernsey as its European production centre because industrial land on the island was cheap. Moonpig is also now an international business with a regional office in Sydney, staffed by the company's former marketing head, an expatriate Australian who wanted to return home.

Nick, who tends to dress pretty smartly, actually looks like an outsider in his own business, given that most of his staff arrive at work dressed down in jeans and T-shirts. He also does a good line in self-deprecation. He told me that he fell into entrepreneurship because he was not bright enough to join the professions. 'It is much easier to give up on your career when you haven't got one,' he told me.

This is not entirely true. After university, Nick worked in the Russian offices of Glencore, a commodities business. He was then involved in a management buy out of the company, which in turn provided him with £600,000 of seed capital to start Moonpig.

Nick exudes calm, despite the many pressures he faced building Moonpig, which required large amounts of upfront investment to get off the ground.

Critically, he knew when to step back and not to meddle when things were tough. During his darkest hour, in March 2001, when a critical £750,000 funding round stalled, putting the company and all of his personal wealth on the line, Nick decided to head for the slopes with friends. 'If this investment hadn't gone through I would have lost everything,' he told me. 'I thought I might as well go on holiday or I would just wear a hole in the carpet.'

This laid-back approach to entrepreneurship perhaps explains why Nick has managed to perpetuate the role of boss without becoming a meddler. The most obvious manifestation of this is in the way he has handed over power. For instance, he relinquished the role of managing director to his former operations head Iain Martin in 2008. 'I felt for one thing I had done all the bits that I needed to do for the business, which was get it off the ground and find the right people to run it,' he told me.

He added that succession was the last thing on his mind when he started the venture. 'Like most entrepreneurs I thought I would start the business and sell it in three years' time,' he said. But having done it, he has the enthusiasm of a religious convert.

Something Nick also displays is an uncanny level of self-awareness about his own managerial limitations. This is vital for a founder if he or she is to realize why he or she needs to hand over responsibility to someone else at a certain stage. 'All of my skills as an entrepreneur are in getting things running,' Nick told me, before adding that he does still see value in being the owner.

'There comes a natural point when a founder CEO needs to hand over. A company has got a life of its own.' One of the reasons that he may have found it easier to hand over the reins was his attitude to work. Many entrepreneurs almost wear their dedication to the office as a badge of honour. This is not necessarily helpful if your workforce then confuses hard work with always being seen in the office, a condition that HR professionals refer to as 'presenteeism'.

There appears to be no danger of this with Nick Jenkins, who refers to the 'shackles' of running a business day to day. At the time of our meeting in 2009 Nick lived beside Battersea Park, a short trip along the River Thames from Moonpig's office. However, he stressed that he only came into the office two or three days a week. He also confided to me that he spent about five weeks a year out of the office pursuing his passion for skiing. He could do this, he said, because he knew there were people back in the office that could make all the important decisions during his absence.

'I have never really worked more than nine to five because it isn't necessary,' he told me. 'A lot of people [who start businesses] find themselves stuffing envelopes for mailshots late into the night, when they could pay someone six quid an hour to do it for them.'

A second lesson from Moonpig is the way that Nick Jenkins has handed over control. Key to the process has been doing it in stages.

His second in command was first made commercial director, then he was given more and more responsibility as he proved himself. 'It is a very difficult step to take,' Nick admitted, adding that he only handed over each department once he was certain his deputy was ready.

This might have been difficult, but Nick smoothed the transition by making sure he was transparent about what was happening and sharing the process with the person taking on the responsibility. 'We sat down and worked it out,' Nick explained, noting that he has kept responsibility for looking after the board. 'I am also there if anything goes wrong, and if anything did go wrong there is an understanding I would step in.'

Another way Nick has stepped back from his business has been to limit his interest to taking decisions on broader issues rather than the nitty-gritty. In doing this, he shows that it is possible to be involved in the business without getting involved in day-to-day decision making.

When I first met him in 2009, he had just returned from a fact-finding mission to Uganda, funded out of his own pocket, to see whether Moonpig could sponsor local children through the charity World Vision. 'There are more satisfying things to spend your money on than expensive watches and flash cars,' he told me.

He claimed the secret to his more liberated lifestyle is to appoint a good management board. 'I have always tried to hire the best people I could,' he said. Perhaps it is the self-effacing character of the British public schoolboys like Nick that enables him to take this stance. For someone with one of the premier brands in the online cards market, Nick is very humble about his business achievements.

He told me that, having freed himself from the 'plate spinning' of running day-to-day operations, his next big move would probably be to start another venture. 'When you have got all of your assets tied up in your business, it is an enormous risk to take, but it is not an enormous risk to bring someone in and gradually hand over assets.'

One of the goals Nick had when we first met was to expand Moonpig into the United States. By the time we next met, a year later, the goal had been achieved. Although the vision was his, it was other people who made the expansion happen. Once again Nick was not the hero, but the heads of his new US operation.

It was a repeat performance of what he had done in pushing Moonpig into Australia a few years previously, and he was aware of the importance of getting others with a better understanding of the local market to do this. 'There is such a cultural difficulty to greetings cards,' he said. 'Australia is a good test-bed for greetings cards because Australians are quite similar to Brits.' He claimed that he was cautious with the Australian expansion in part because it is extremely easy to alienate customers in another country.

Nick also had an example to show how easy it is for a founder to make the wrong call as a company expands in an anecdote about the time he decided to run Moonpig's British advertising campaign on Australian television. The film, which was a hit in the UK, showed the company's cards being put on a fireplace, so the decision was taken to use it again down under. Sadly, the message was lost on its audience in the sunny south Pacific, for whom fireplaces are anathema. After that, Nick told me he learnt his lesson about getting an Australian marketing expert to lead the local campaign.

The process of handing over to a new foreign operation is handled carefully at Moonpig. In the case of the US expansion, it was a matter of making sure there was an American in the London office, whose job was to work out what would work in terms of card design in the US market.

Nick clearly still enjoys being involved in his corporate baby, albeit at arm's length. Unlike the meddling entrepreneurs that David Molian described to me, Nick has not lost interest in his venture. By moving beyond being a hero for his enterprise, he seems to have retained both the interest in his business and the freedom to consider new ventures. 'A lot of people who start a business confuse their own personal freedom with an exit,' he explained. 'There is nothing stopping me from pursuing other things. That is one of the joys of stepping back a bit.'

Cranfield's tutors have a phrase for this way of thinking. 'Working on the business, not in the business.'

Stepping back from the business gives you time to think about strategy, according to Nick. 'I spend a lot of my time thinking about things,' he says. 'I do go researching.' He also tries to get out of the entrepreneur bubble that has appeared in the London start-up community, similar to the one that exists in other cluster cities, such as San Francisco and Berlin.

Entrepreneurs are no different in this sense from other people and tend to hang out with people who do a similar job or with whom they share a workplace. Nick is a personal friend of several other successful internet entrepreneurs in London, such as Michael Acton Smith, founder of the online gadget shop Firebox.com and the hugely successful social network for children, Moshi Monsters. However, he told me he tended to network informally with those who have started businesses in other sectors, often at business seminars. 'It is quite useful to say I did this kind of activity and it didn't work,' he said. 'We swap our stories.'

Confessions of a meddler

Of course, not everyone is born with such good leadership skills. The good news is that it is possible to change your ways.

Guy Chatburn is another Brit involved in a business using the latest technology to update a service traditionally provided through the postal service born in the Victorian era. He is managing director of Send Marketing, a direct mail business based in the West Midlands. Unlike Nick Jenkins, however, Guy told me he was a self-confessed hero for many years and a bit of a meddler to boot. 'There are always last-minute client issues,' he explained. 'When you had fixed one problem, someone else comes along with other ones.'

Guy's obsession with being involved in every decision meant that for a long while he was the first in the office and the last one out. He admitted to me that his obsession with micro-managing meant he did not take a holiday for three years after creating his company. It was only when a fellow entrepreneur told him that he needed to bring in outside help that the penny dropped, he said.

Fortunately, Guy acted. He found someone to be his operations director who had worked at a larger direct mail business that he aspired to mimic. This connection, Guy claims, gave him the confidence to delegate responsibility to the new senior executive from day one. 'Being a hero, I was always creating lots of rules and regulations,' he told me. 'He said this is how we did it [at the rival business] and I thought if it works with them, then just do it.' The result was improved quality control and higher customer satisfaction, according to Guy.

It also freed him up to focus on sales and marketing. This resulted in a new product aimed at smaller businesses that enabled them to have direct mail printed, put in an envelope and sent out for 27 p apiece. At the time of the launch in 2008, this was the cost of a second-class stamp, a price Send Marketing could get by buying its postage in bulk from one of the alternative carriers to Royal Mail, the UK's incumbent carrier. When Royal Mail raised the price of postage in 2009, Send Marketing was able to maintain its 27 p per item price.

It was this ability to undercut the conventional means of distribution that helped Send Marketing to more than treble its client base that year. This efficiency proved critical following the financial crisis of 2008 as some of Send Marketing's more established larger customers cut back on direct mail to save money.

At the time, there was a question mark over whether Guy would be able to afford to step back from the business, but he made the leap anyway. 'It cost me a lot [to hire the operations director] because it was a very senior salary, but I have more than recouped that,' he told me.

It was this decision to hand over powers, that finally removed Guy from exerting his hero tendencies and he has changed his ways as a result, he told me.

However, breaking old habits can be tough.

Alex Smith founded Alara, an organic muesli business, from a central London squat in 1975. The company had grown into a wholesale manufacturing and retail operation when I met him in 2009, when it had an annual turnover of £5 m and had just grown by 20 per cent in 12 months. Alex claimed at the time that he was quite happy with the company's growth, except when he compared himself with the smoothie maker Innocent Drinks, another London-based ethical food business, which had grown much faster than Alara in far less time.

'It is definitely still a road I am travelling down,' Alex said, referring to the need to hand on more control, which he appeared to be accepting in theory but not in practice. Alex claimed the reason he found it so difficult to remove himself from day-to-day activities was that, like many entrepreneurial heroes, he felt he had locked all the knowledge about doing the work in his head. 'Because I am so intimately involved in the business, I have an instinctive understanding of what to do,' he told me. As a result, Alex had to create structures along the way to ensure that others could understand what he has been doing. He admitted at the time we spoke that he believed he would be able to think about new ventures if he was able to become less of a hero at Alara. 'I am getting closer and closer to it,' he said.

Not every founder agrees, however, that playing the hero is a bad thing.

David Macken, whom I spoke to at about the same time as Alex, ran System Associates, a software and internet hosting business he and his partner acquired in a management buyout in 2003. At the time, he was trying to cut down the long hours he spent at the company. However, he insisted that rolling up your sleeves every now and then was not a bad thing for his company, where there were just 20 people on the payroll. 'In a small business, it is unrealistic to expect that you can be purely a manager,' he said. 'Occasionally there is something challenging that requires some very long hours.'

System Associates' clients are public sector bodies, such as the British Library, HM Treasury and the Department of Work and

Pensions. According to Dave, it is not uncommon to get a call from one at 5 pm, asking to get a new section of a website up and running before an announcement the next day on *Today*, BBC Radio Four's morning news programme. 'If I added an extra three or four people [to handle these demands], then the business would be less profitable,' he told me.

Part of the reason many entrepreneurs take on the meddler mantle is because they feel they have to be the sole champion of the business. This is partly due to the way some cultures raise the character of a founder above the many other people needed to make a start-up achieve considerable success.

In the United States, this tends to be more extreme. Founders are often treated like celebrities, which can be both good for the image of entrepreneurship and bad for those who take it up thinking that they alone will guide their venture to success. Steve Jobs, Bill Gates and Mark Zuckerberg have all received this treatment, but none of their enterprises (Apple, Microsoft and Facebook) would ever have become the internationally successful businesses they now are without a team of people. These celebrity entrepreneurs may seem to have been gifted with the genes to grow such large companies, but the truth is that they too have had to develop from founders into leaders who can manage multibillion dollar companies employing thousands of people. In Steve Jobs's case, he actually left the company for a period, only to return a renewed man, partly because of the influence other people had had upon him. Many other founders have failed this test of developing with their business and their companies have withered on the vine.

Although the UK still has its celebrity entrepreneurs, this cult of the leader seems to be less strong in a culture that appears to prefer failure to success, and with heroes who are only too aware of the chinks in their armour.

Sir James Dyson, creator of the bagless vacuum cleaner and bladeless fan, is a prime example. Sir James is one of the UK's best known founders. He also happens to be an inventor as well. However, he passed on the baton of control of his business to one of his employees, Martin McCourt, in 2001, and then chose to take on the title 'chief engineer'. In spite of the column inches devoted to entrepreneurs that are presented as one-man dynamos, able to lead a venture from start to finish, most founders across the world follow the Dyson route.

I have found this consistently in my time writing about entrepreneurs in people like Marco Schiavo, founder of Salt, a recruitment business for software programmers. He told me that he decided to recruit a professional managing director, partly so that he could spend time on other projects, but also because he recognized that companies need different expertise at different stages of growth. This is exactly why founders should step back from being the heroes of their companies.

This has not stopped others, particularly in the venture capital community, continuing to seek the founder who can grow into a bigger leadership role as their business empire expands. Andreessen Horowitz, a $300m venture fund based in Menlo Park, California, openly admits in its literature to a bias for 'founder CEOs', noting that these people are far more likely to have the creative spark to spot the future opportunities for their business. While external chief executives are often better at maximizing product cycles, this skill can be taught, co-founder Ben Horowitz told me.

Saul Klein, the Lovefilm founder we heard about in the last chapter, is another supporter of the founder as chief executive. He is now a partner at venture capital group Index Ventures, one of the big investors in technology start-ups, with operations in the United States, Europe and Israel. Saul said he likes to back companies with founders at the helm. 'There is no reason why, if you are open minded and determined to learn and develop, you can have no management experience or expertise and still be ten times a better CEO than a so-called professional manager,' he told me. 'I think the most interesting founders to back are the ones who have the desire and the potential to go all the way,' he added. 'They may not, and many won't, but that doesn't change the fact that that is the person you want.'

This does not mean that Saul thinks only founder-run businesses are worth investing in, which perhaps says something about the rarity of these kinds of people. Only 15 out of every 100 investments he makes are put into companies run by founder chief executives.

Saul himself is an example of a founder who has handed on the baton, having helped install Simon Calver, a senior executive at Dell and PepsiCo among other places, as chief executive of Lovefilm.

Saul admits that there is a certain mythology about the importance of chief executives, which plays down the importance of founders who remain with their start-up but not at its head. 'Someone has to be made accountable for making a final decision, but at the end of the day no CEO makes that decision on his or her own. Running a business is always a team game.'

An exception to the rule

There are always exceptions to any rule. And it is true that some founders do manage to take their company to much greater heights.

Richard Moross is founder of Moo.com, which, like Moonpig, uses the advances of online technology to allow people to create customized business cards and other stationery. It too is based in London. In fact it was one of the first technology companies to locate to the Shoreditch region of the city that has since become a magnet for such enterprises, earning itself the monicker Silicon Roundabout.

Richard has taken Moo.com from the first days, where he was ordering pizza for his programmers, to its current state as a multi-national business. The difference now is that he spends a large chunk of his time presenting slides to his board of directors rather than busying himself with operational details. Other people have been hired to do the day-to-day stuff, and it is a credit to Richard that he gives them the authority to do this.

He is now considered a leading player in the Silicon Roundabout cluster of companies, providing a home to other start-ups in his office space.

However, Richard insists he still feels comfortable being in charge of his own venture day to day. 'There is a huge advantage to having a strong thread from the beginning of the company to the end,' he told me, noting that it would be difficult to pass on the level of knowledge he has of the company and its customers to another person.

What he also believes is that founders need to continue learning if they are to develop into people who can run much larger operations. Richard told me he has gained a great deal of help from the Young Presidents' Organisation, a global network of 17,000 business heads in more than 100 countries, whose mission is to build better leaders through education and the exchange of ideas. He said that support from other YPO members has increased his confidence in his ability to achieve his goal of leading Moo.com to far greater heights than it has so far reached.

Founder chief executives are a lot more common than some people think, according to Richard. If we don't see them it might be because they don't believe their role is to seek the limelight. 'It is obvious in some companies because they are led by people with magnetic personalities,' he said. 'However, there are plenty of other successful companies where the founder chief executive just keeps a lower profile.'

As I have said, my experience in talking to a wide range of founders and investors would tend to suggest otherwise. However, the fact that those founders who are still chief executives of their businesses are keeping a low profile suggests that they are also willing to give others the limelight within their companies, a sure sign they are not displaying hero tendencies.

When do you step back?

A key part of avoiding the temptation to be a hero is to know when to step back.

Most entrepreneurs understand that they need to take time out from day-to-day operations to build their businesses. Many fail to achieve this. The theory that you build a team of experts around you to take over the day-to-day running of the business often falls apart if the founder struggles to delegate responsibility.

For Debra Charles, this process was particularly hard because her smart card business, Novacroft, held so many personal connections. The death of both her parents had provided Debra with both the spur and the funding to launch Novacroft from her kitchen table in 1998. The name Novacroft was borrowed from her mother Dorothy's kennels business, and the inheritance provided the seed capital to get the business off the ground. 'I just thought life is short, so I need to make this a reality,' she told me.

The Northampton-based business now manages more than a million customer records for clients that issue pre-paid travel tickets and other smart cards. It operates a customer call centre just outside the city, and clients include Transport for London, for which it operates the concessionary Oyster card scheme for students, children and 16- and 17-year-olds.

Although Debra managed to grow the business to a multi million pound operation, she admitted to me that she struggled to let go. 'There was a point where 20-odd managers were reporting directly to me,' she explains. 'There was no one looking ahead to where the business was going.'

The spur for Debra was attending Cranfield's BGP course. She returned to the office and drew up a list of her business's key functions and then built a senior management team consisting of people assigned to each role. Only one of these appointments did not work out, although Debra told me it made her realize that the recruitment process was key to building the necessary trust in the people she appointed.

Regular communication remains critical, she said, adding that she holds weekly meetings with her team.

When I spoke to Debra, she had had a model soccer pitch set up in her office to show how she managed the business, which had grown by 50 per cent in the year since she made the changes. The problem in the past, Debra explained to me, was that she was playing with the rest of her team at the far end of the pitch. What she wanted was for her managers to think about playing in the midfield, where they could handle operational problems while planning for the future needs of the business, such as IT investments.

She said she saw her position as near to the opposition's goal, providing the vision for the rest of her team to follow. 'I don't understand all the rules of football, but I am a visual person and I like the idea of seeing my team on a pitch,' she said.

The experience of Debra and her business demonstrates the problems facing an owner-manager who is intimately linked with a venture. Adam King of King & Allen, a London-based bespoke tailoring service, told me that not knowing how to make suits has made him a better owner-manager. 'I am no tailor, nor will I ever be,' he said. 'Of course there are day-to-day things that I'm dragged into but I've never been heavily involved in them as the business plan never got me involved in the first place.'

Duncan Cheatle has met hundreds of entrepreneurs through his networking business The Supper Club. He told me that few people have the energy to build a business with more than £1m revenue without taking time away from daily operational matters.

Like all successful founders, Duncan has himself worked long hours to make his business a success. However, he also told me he is a big fan of foreign holidays to relax the mind, or just socializing with friends who can challenge his thinking. 'If you stay in your office with your colleagues, you will just solve the same problems,' he said. 'There is something about removing yourself, even getting abroad, that enables you to clear your head to get that breakthrough idea.'

Duncan also promotes taking time away from communications technology. 'There is too much buzz,' he told me. 'You need that space where you are not being assaulted by e-mail, phones and texts.'

One entrepreneur who sought to do something about this across one of his businesses was John Caudwell, founder of, among other businesses, phones4u, one of the UK's largest mobile phone retail chains. In 2004, he caused a sensation by announcing that he would ban e-mail from the workplace. In spite of the media hype at the time, the ban was very short-lived and the company later insisted it was intended to draw employee attention to the fact that some people were spending hours a day trawling through unnecessary e-mail. However, it sought to highlight a useful point about the draw of new media and the risk to productivity that obsessive texting, e-mailing and social networking can present.

External factors are important too

The reasons people find it hard to hand over control are many and varied. It may not just be due to the personalities of the founders but the circumstances in which they came to be running the business.

Andy Mindel and his brother Mike, two north London entrepreneurs, first went into business as custodians of their father's photograph storage business, Arrowfile. It was the late 1990s and the brothers were fresh out of college. It was also the time of the first wave of internet businesses and picture-sharing websites were popping up, making Arrowfile's business model look redundant.

Mike and Andy managed to sell Arrowfile but the trauma of ditching the business their father had spent most of his working life growing clearly left some scars. 'We know what it is like to sell a business; we just don't want to go through that again,' Andy told me when I first met with them in 2007 to discuss their next venture, Wordtracker. It was clear at the time that they had learnt one thing from their experience – the internet was the place to create fast-growing businesses with some durability. Wordtracker pinpointed the best words for online businesses to use to attract people making internet searches.

At the time of our first meeting, the brothers were running the business in a small office near to the Kentish Town home where they had started it. The business was in its ninth year and had just made a £492,000 profit on a turnover of £1.3 m. This might not be bad for some start-ups, but in a market where Google had become one of the world's largest companies the Mindel brothers clearly had some work to do. As it turned out, it might just have been that they were good at founding companies but not so good at growing them. However, there they were still at the helm.

When I next caught up with them three years later the brothers had made serious inroads into replacing themselves and stepping back from day-to-day operations. They had hired managers for both the technical and commercial side of the company and were handing over responsibilities. At the time, however, they were both still displaying the classic trauma of founders struggling to give up control over the thing they had created. 'When something is your baby and you have been part of this thing for so long, it becomes hard to trust people to do things,' Andy said. Having done it, however, they were both clearly glad to have taken a step back from the business.

Like Nick Jenkins at Moonpig, the brothers handed over responsibility slowly. Mike, for instance, remained chief technology officer for another couple of years. In their case, the process of withdrawal was handled so gently that it became difficult at first to see when they had actually stopped being involved in the day-to-day decision making. 'It got to a point where we said, hang on a minute, we can actually stand back,' Andy said.

Having made the move, however, Andy said he was already seeing the benefits in terms of being able to network more widely and look at the business more strategically. In the six months since he had withdrawn from his managerial role, he noted that he had been able to launch a couple of new research tools, taking the business in new directions. 'My only regret is that I didn't make this move sooner,' Andy told me at the time.

Wind the clock forward another year, and Mike had also worked his way out of daily operations, handing over his chief technology officer's role and becoming instead a non-executive director. At the same time, he had been taking on new projects, including helping to make a feature film, a process he said was very similar to a start-up.

Mike had also launched a new online business with Andy, this time buying up profitable websites, using their skills in web search optimization to improve the companies' revenues and selling them on. 'I am a start-up guy,' Mike admitted, adding that he had finally stepped back from Wordtracker because he realized that he couldn't run this more mature company the way he wanted to. Part of what he enjoyed was the buzz and the camaraderie and he admitted that this was difficult to maintain when a company reached a certain size.

Richard Salvage is a British entrepreneur who sold his first business in 2006. He then moved on to control a group of businesses, each managed by other people, under the umbrella company Medsa Group. As such he could satisfy his desire to be a founder and strategist while running a much larger business operation.

The three key elements to becoming a strategist (a healthy state of leadership) rather than a meddler in a business are to have good processes, mechanisms to measure those processes and the right calibre of people, he told me.

> If you want to work on the business, you can only do it with support. You have to recognize that your management team shares the same culture and same expectations as you have and that can manifest itself in some measurable outputs.

The toughest part is always getting the right people to deliver on your behalf, Richard added. One common mistake is to assume that someone with a good track record in a large company is going to be good in a smaller growing business. Not only is it a lot easier to perform well when your company has a strong brand, but people who have been in a large business often find it hard to settle into a company where everyone has to muck in.

We will return to this topic in more detail in a later chapter in regard to sales heads.

However, suffice it to say that making the right senior appointment is crucial when it comes to any senior role because of the high cost of hiring the wrong person. Silver Fleet, a third-generation family business running dinner cruises on the River Thames, was almost brought to its knees by a general manager who did not work out as expected. 'We didn't do our proper due diligence,' managing director Tom Woods told me. 'That led to four years of hell.'

The experience marked Tom because at the time he was preparing to take up ownership of the business from his father. It later returned to haunt him after his sales head of eight years decided to take a career break after the birth of her first child. Tom was concerned that he would pick a candidate because he clicked with that person on a social level, only to find that he'd picked someone who was not right for the role. This was the mistake he made before.

To avoid repeating history, he employed CBSL People, a specialist HR consultancy, to help him through the process. 'They interviewed me to find out what I wanted in the role,' Tom said to me. 'By talking it through, it exposed the holes in my preparation.' CBSL helped Tom with writing the job advertisements, ensuring that the business owner neither undersold nor oversold the position. It also vetted the CVs and briefed Tom on the interview structure.

Tom whittled 100 potential candidates down to a shortlist of six. He admitted to me that in the past he may have put too much emphasis on whether he got on with such a person. 'One of the most important things I have realized is, while I am looking for chemistry with the applicant, it is secondary to whether they can do the job,' he said.

As a business journalist, I realize how the media has contributed to the mythical cult of the lone founder. The story of an exceptional individual who succeeds against the odds makes a better narrative than a long explanation of all the people who really made a certain brand work. Newspaper readers like a personality interview with the chief executive of a business. However, the danger of these pieces is that they suggest a company's success is the result of one person's expertise alone.

The truth is often more difficult to explain than is possible in a 900-word feature. Hopefully this chapter has gone some way towards redressing that balance.

The conclusion

The key message of this chapter is to be aware that as founder you may not be the best person to take a business forward beyond a certain size, often around the 50-person mark.

The problem is that charismatic founders, so important in the early days of a start-up, can so often turn into meddlers when the business reaches a certain scale.

While it is possible for founders to evolve into strategic leaders, and there are leadership and coaching groups to help in this process, it is often necessary to bring in another person with the particular skills to manage a company's next stage of growth.

This does not mean that you need to step down as the head of a company, but it probably does mean your changing your role in the company.

It may also help to realize that handing over the reins of a business does not have to be done suddenly. In fact, all the examples in this chapter look at people who have gradually passed over responsibility, making sure the new chief can handle one piece of power before handing over the next.

The good news for anyone who finds that they have become a meddler is that it is never too late to change your ways. It may be the best thing you have ever done for your business.

Chapter Four
The high price of success

Oscar Wilde famously said: 'A cynic knows the price of everything, and the value of nothing.' Evidently, he was not an entrepreneur.

The price you charge for a product can be the rocket fuel to enable your venture to expand exponentially with the minimum of effort, or it can be a millstone that can put people off and make the cost of customer acquisition more expensive. The problem is that pricing is hard to get right and easy to undervalue. It can also be paradoxical.

The trouble with pricing is that it is not as straightforward as other management decisions. When it comes to staffing, service levels or product quality, the goal is always easy – aim for the best. But what do you do with pricing? Do you want the price that maximizes sales growth to create an even larger business or the highest profit for your company at this particular moment? Often these are conflicting goals.

It is actually more complicated than that because the relationship between the price you charge and the profits you make is affected by the costs you incur. If you are a manufacturer you have to take into account reject rates, the cost of maintaining your machines, rent, insurance and your inventory costs. You might own a car-parts business that specializes in carrying older parts for classic cars. You might pride yourself on having the head cylinder gasket for every

Triumph sports car made since 1958, and believe that you can charge a premium for that level of availability. But what kind of a premium can you charge for that? What is the cost of carrying such a large inventory?

Less can be more

The mistake many business owners succumb to is the belief that they need to keep their prices as low as possible to support strong growth. This obsession is usually driven by a misguided sales director, who believes that his or her target should be to sell more of everything.

As the boss, however, you are probably more concerned about maximizing the profit. Cheap may well be an enticing prospect for us as consumers. But if you are the business owner, the reality is that if you sell at a low price, you are getting less money for every item you sell. You therefore not only have to produce more of whatever you produce, but you have to spend more time finding people to sell your wares to in order to make a decent profit – after all, your margins will be lower on every item sold. If you are lucky enough to find more willing buyers, you will then have to spend yet more money getting the goods or service to them. This cost of acquisition may well wipe out any gain you are making from selling the product.

Do the mathematics

I have to warn you now that this chapter does involve some mathematics. It may seem tiresome, but it is the best way to explain the relationship of price and sales.

A good place to start is a break-even analysis on any potential price increases. Suppose you have a gross margin of 36 per cent, but that margin does not leave enough money to cover your overheads and provide a profit.

If you increase prices by 2 per cent, you will have to lose more than 5 per cent of your sales to lose money on the change. If you lose only 2 per cent of sales, you will have about the same revenue but your costs of goods sold will fall by 2 per cent as well. That might be enough to enable you to start making money. It will also mean less work because you have fewer transactions.

For example, say you sell 100 widgets a week at £100 apiece and they cost you £65 each to make. This will give you a gross profit of £35 a widget or £3,500 a week. Because you think these are really high-quality widgets, you decide you can charge £102. If you now sell only 95 widgets a week you will have a gross profit of £3,515 (95 multiplied by 37). If you manage to sell 98, then you will make £3,626.

The point is that demand will have to fall by quite a bit for you not to come out ahead from a price rise.

However, price is not just a matter of improving the profit and loss account in your business ledger. When you lower your prices you are also sending out a message about the value of your goods.

What your prices say about the value of your offering

We may all like to think we are rational beings who are not led astray by the price tag on a sofa or a suit, but psychologists will tell us otherwise. The amount people pay will affect their attitude to whatever they are buying.

To turn around the Wildean quote at the head of this chapter, a low price also carries with it the risk that you will present the image to potential customers that your product is not really very valuable. This will in turn make it harder still to convince more people to buy from you. And if you cannot sell more products or services, you will struggle to make a profit.

Why you need to keep prices up

Of course some very successful businesses have made a virtue out of providing the lowest price.

The kings of this strategy in recent years have been the budget airline operators – first Southwest Airlines in the United States, and later (in a direct copy of the business model, as we saw in Chapter 2) by Ryanair in Europe. These go-getting businesses have been very entrepreneurial in the way they have disrupted a market by changing the business model. They have grabbed market share from the lumbering dinosaurs of the air travel market (the national carriers), in large part by lowering the cost of flying for the general public.

However, in the process they have also reduced the cachet of flying. This might not be an issue for Ryanair or Southwest Airlines, but it is worth looking at in relation to how price can affect an industry. The days when people would put on their best clothes to travel to the airport have long passed. We might be able to fly more than we used to, but it is not a valued experience now that Michael O'Leary, chief executive of Ryanair, has exposed the truth about air travel: that it is a coach journey with wings.

Mr O'Leary has in fact taken the low-price model to such extremes that it is having to create prices for parts of the service customers previously considered free, such as going to the toilet mid-flight. It has been a similar story in the supermarket sector. Whether it is Tesco in the UK or Walmart in the United States, these food retailers have perfected the art of peddling us cheap food. The problem with these beggar-thy-neighbour pricing strategies is that there can only be one winner, and the chances are that that one company will have to be bigger than everyone else.

At best it is probably a short-term policy to try to charge the lowest price. Even disruptive business models that enter a market extolling their low prices end up raising them in order to achieve more value. I will explain how this happened in Jamie Murray Wells's Glasses Direct later in this book. Suffice it to say for now, there is no economic logic in these companies charging a certain low price when customers are willing to pay much more without a significant reduction in demand.

The supermarket sector also shows us how charging a high price in a market can be a good idea even when competitors are slashing their prices in a race to the bottom. Waitrose, the favourite grocer to the UK's middle classes, has made a virtue out of focusing on the quality of goods it offers rather than the cost of buying them. It might not be as large as its British competitors, Tesco, Asda and Sainsbury's, all of which compete on price, but it is a very profitable business. It has also proved more resilient than its rivals to the downturn in consumer spending in recent years.

Warren Buffett, whose nickname 'the sage of Omaha' has been hard earned through years of consistent investment success, summed up the issue of price in relation to a company's value when he said: 'It's far better to buy a wonderful company at a fair price than a fair company at a wonderful price.' What he meant was that you need to aim to be the best, and price accordingly. This is about building your value so the fair price is attractive because the offering is desirable.

The difficult relationship between price and value

The relationship between price and perceived quality is not a straightforward one, however. A high-quality item sold at a high price can confer status, while the same item sold at a low price is a super-bargain. Both purchases are something customers might tell their friends about. Even terminology can make a difference. Describing something as 'affordable' or 'good value' can create a different impression from describing it as 'cheap'.

Rebel entrepreneurs prized for their wisdom when it comes to value use their prices to display something more than the cost of providing it. They realize that the price is a way of controlling demand, but it is also a way of building a cachet about brand.

Take John Smedley, the British luxury knitwear manufacturer. This family-owned business, based in the strikingly beautiful surroundings of Derbyshire's Derwent Valley, is the most experienced rebel entrepreneur this book presents. It has been operating its looms for almost 230 years – longer, it is believed, than any other mass manufacturer of any product anywhere in the world. Just 13 years after Richard Arkwright completed his first water-powered spinning mill at the dawn of the Industrial Revolution, Peter Nightingale and his associate John Smedley set up their knitting machines next door in the building the current management still uses today. When I was taken around the site by the then manager Drew Walker, he showed me a cornerstone on an outbuilding with 1784 on it, making the property only a little younger than the US constitution.

John Smedley is a company that has more experience of capitalism than almost any other business trading at the moment, so perhaps it has some lessons for the rest of us on the subject of price. Its founders started at the bottom (literally, producing knitted underwear), but progressed quickly up the value chain to posh outer garments. Despite the temptation to go down market and perhaps pick up sales from a much broader range of clientele in need of hosiery, it stuck with the luxury trade. There is a good reason for this, which I will come to later.

The business also believed in spending money to make money. Its early research and development work enabled John Smedley to take the credit for several early innovations in modern fashion, such as the twin set, a combination of cardigan and jumper beloved by tweedy aristocrats and those that aspire to be such. The business has continued to show a very British nous for creating cutting-edge garments that nevertheless look like they have been made that way for generations.

Despite its age, John Smedley remains a highly entrepreneurial business, partly because, while family owned, it has not been afraid to hand control of the board to non-family members if the right candidate comes along. Those family members who are involved on the board also display a fair bit of entrepreneurial flair themselves. For instance, Ian Maclean, a seventh-generation family board member, started out as an investment manager at venture capital firm 3i Group.

The team in charge of John Smedley at the moment are also very sophisticated in the way they use price. The company's garments certainly cost a pretty penny to make. The merino wool used to produce its fine-gauge knitted jumpers are shipped halfway round the world from specific farms in New Zealand. The sea island cotton in the lighter, summer garments is equally carefully sourced. Little touches like knowing the exact farm where every piece of wool comes from adds to the cachet of the brand, but they do not come cheap. The thing is that the £100-plus you pay for a John Smedley pullover, while not insignificant, bears little connection with the price of making the goods.

Price for John Smedley is a tool to help maintain its image as a luxury brand in the 35 or so countries around the world where its products are sold. 'Made in England' may not appeal to many in terms of mass-produced goods, but in luxury it has become highly prized. And John Smedley needs those international markets. The UK might still be home to the business, but this small island in the Atlantic Ocean only accounts for 30 per cent of the sales. It is eclipsed by the company's largest market, Japan. Americans also snap up whatever John Smedley has to offer as the company has ridden the wave of the fascination with British design and fashion brands, alongside Burberry, Aquascutum and Dunhill. The target customer in all these markets is a person of above average wealth. There might be only a few of these people in any one country, but across the world they make a more than big enough market for John Smedley to build a substantial and profitable business.

To John Smedley's target consumers, price is a mark of exclusivity that keeps them ahead of the Joneses, Sakamotos and Clintons. The high price therefore confers status on the shopper who can afford it.

A high price is much more than a branding exercise at John Smedley. It is also about good husbandry of the raw materials needed to make the knitwear, as well as maintaining levels of service and managing the bottom line. Part of the brand of John Smedley, after all, is its reliability and exclusivity. If too many people wore John Smedley garments, the company might be unable to keep up with the high demands of its customers. Even with the addition of state-of-the-art Japanese knitting machinery to the Derbyshire factory a few years ago, the company's managing director admits that quality would suffer if the business tried to produce any more than 500,000 garments a year.

For John Smedley, therefore, the high price enables it to maintain its brand in two ways: firstly, as a luxury fashion garment and, secondly, in controlling supply so the quality threshold is not breached. It looks unlikely, therefore, that John Smedley is going to change its decades-old pricing policy any time soon.

In a recession, the need to raise prices only increases

But what about growing companies, trying to break into a new market? Can they really demand high prices when nobody knows about their product or trusts it?

Or what about when there is a recession? Surely then a smart entrepreneur would want to lower prices to attract the few people left with money to spend? Not according to many of those who have been there and succeeded.

Alan Burgess runs Masterframe Windows, a manufacturer of U-PVC sash windows. His business is trying to walk a difficult line, selling into a premium market with a product (U-PVC) that many house-holders, particularly in tradition-loving Britain, feel is inferior.

Everything about this business seems a long way from the high-rolling world of people who shop for John Smedley garments.

Masterframe Windows is considerably younger than John Smedley, having been started only a couple of decades ago. The business is also based in Essex, a county known to the British more for its lack of taste than for quality craftsmanship. If all that were not enough, Masterframe Windows is operating in a market (house building) that was paralysed by the 2008 financial crisis. Those house builders that have survived the shake-out are keen to save costs wherever possible. So how could a company like Masterframe Windows survive?

In such circumstances the obvious thing for Alan to have done would have been to lower his prices to increase demand, thus boosting his turnover. But that is the exact opposite of what he did. 'Our opening line is that we are the most expensive U-PVC sash window manufacturer in the UK,' he told me cheerily. 'You either get a click and the phone goes dead, which touch wood has never happened, or you get a question: "Why is that?"'

Taking such a position may make sense to an ambitious entrepreneur like Alan – Essex men are raised with a strong sense of self-belief. However, he also has concrete proof that his strategy of raising prices has worked. During the depths of the recession just gone, Masterframe's annual turnover actually increased, helping the company to not only survive but grow while competitors perished.

However, the strategy of raising prices in a downturn still takes nerves of steel.

A couple of years ago, Masterframe's largest customer, a national house builder that accounts for a fifth of the company's revenue, set up a reverse auction for renewal of the contract in an effort to shave costs. Alan told me that he not only refused to cut his prices, he submitted the highest bill of the six tenders offered.

The customer could have saved £250,000 by taking the cheapest bid, but it declined to do so after Alan convinced the buyers that Masterframe's product was the best. 'It was scary as hell,' Alan recalled, adding that the customer was eventually swayed by its own market tests, where three-quarters of its sample chose Masterframe's sash windows over cheaper rival designs even when they knew they would have to pay twice as much. In the 24 months after the auction was called, the customer increased its orders from Masterframe by 50 per cent. 'We played bluff and they blinked,' Alan said.

Alan believes that focusing on the quality of the product rather than the cost has been key to the success of Masterframe, which now claims a 15 per cent share of its market for replacement windows. However, convincing customers of the logic of buying a more expensive product has been no mean feat. In the construction industry, everyone tries to sell their products and services on the basis of price, which inevitably leads to a race to the bottom. Homeowners have been taught that if they want a building job done they should get at least three quotes and compare them as if everyone providing the work was the same.

Positioning Masterframe's sash windows as a premium product became critical as the economy went into decline.

Two sorts of businesses do really well in a recession: the big retailers, which stack them high to sell them cheap, thus offering consumers a bargain, and the branded products, because the people who buy them are not affected by recession. Although Masterframe did not act to undermine its pricing policy, it did have to change its focus slightly as a business. One of the most difficult decisions for Alan, who shares 100 per cent ownership of Masterframe with his wife Linda, was to move away from selling to independent builders, who are price sensitive, and to focus on consumers and window installers. 'In the past we have gone into new-build work and have been bitten,' he said.

Masterframe had a turnover of about £5 m in 2000, but it fell by a third when Mr Burgess decided it would no longer target the building industry alone. 'It changed the shape of our business, but it was absolutely the right thing to do,' he said.

When I spoke to Alan in 2008, Masterframe was getting about half of its turnover from domestic window purchases, through its Bygone Collection brand, and just over a third from a network of window installers. Convincing the installers that higher prices are good for business has also been a challenge, Alan admitted. He recalled to me the shock on one Cornish window fitter's face when he told him that Masterframe would increase its price from £500 to £550 per window. 'He said there is no way that people in Cornwall will buy at that price. Now he cannot fit enough windows.'

Alan told me that a significant part of his job is to educate installers such as these, so that they can sell to their clients on the quality of the windows rather than the price. Masterframe's £120,000 marketing budget, which used to be spent on trade shows, has been redirected to educating installers and the public about the importance of quality in building materials.

A few years ago Alan attended Cranfield University's BGP course. The course, as has already been mentioned, is designed specifically for ambitious entrepreneurs like Alan, and he was so inspired that he worked with the business school to create a version of the course for Masterframe's network of installers to attend.

'The trade market is fickle,' he told me. 'So what we need to find is a network of installers out there that know the product, love the product and are capable of expanding the business.' Alan markets the Masterframe brand by buying exhibition space at consumer events such as the Grand Designs show held at London's Excel conference centre, an upmarket show aimed at those with the money to consider building their own home from scratch. He uses such events to highlight the quality of Masterframe's products to home-owners interested in installing traditional sash windows to their property but unwilling to put up with the old technology of wooden frames.

'We have now got timber window suppliers wanting our products,' he told me, adding that many people struggle to tell the difference between Masterframe's U-PVC product and real wood. Well he would do, wouldn't he? But the high price of Masterframe's products may well help the argument that this is no average product. The pressure to keep prices high is likely to only increase for Alan.

Changes in fashion and the quality of construction mean that the sash window market has shrunk by 20 per cent in the past four years, he told me. However, this rebel entrepreneur shows no signs of giving up the fight. 'We are in a dying market, but we have grown significantly,' he says.

The art of maintaining a high price

Of course, raising prices is not always such a conscious decision, but it always has to be handled carefully. To misquote Shakespeare's character Malvolio in *Twelfth Night*: some companies are born with high prices, some achieve high prices and some have high prices thrust upon them.

The sharp decline in sterling's value against other currencies after the financial crisis meant that Lingo 24, an Aberdeen-based online translation service, had to cut rates for the thousands of overseas translators it uses, and raise prices for its UK-based customers. In both cases, the company chose to personalize the message and found a way to present the bad news as a positive development for all, according to Christian Arno, Lingo 24's founder.

For customers, the price increases were presented as a sign of the premium quality of Lingo 24's service. 'It gave clients flexibility,' Christian told me. 'If pricing was an issue, they could go to a different service level.' He explained that the business spoke specifically to its 100 largest clients and did not lose one. In fact, the month after it raised prices saw the company's best revenue figures since it was founded almost eight years earlier, in true rebel entrepreneur style, in Christian's bedroom.

Communicating with staff was potentially more complex. Lingo 24 has 100 full-time employees, but uses the services of more than 3,000 translators, 80 per cent of whom live outside the UK. Christian got his communications head to draft a single e-mail explaining that pay rates were being cut by 10 per cent and outlining the reasons for doing this. Each project manager would then personalize this for the translators under his or her jurisdiction. 'We made sure, where we could, we found a benefit for the translator,' Christian explained to me. Like other freelancers, translators value the volume of work more highly than the hourly rate, so Lingo 24 tried to offer a guaranteed quantity of work each month. In some cases, it was also able to offer faster payment.

Christian admitted that he was lucky to have other people in his company to communicate his message. 'The entrepreneurs I know are generally quite good at ideas but not very good at execution,' he said. 'What was really fortunate for us was that I wasn't actually doing this process and the guys that took it on were very sensitive to the people they were talking to.'

Another entrepreneur who was forced into raising prices was Ryan Notz. Ryan is not just a rebel entrepreneur, but a maverick. He is an American who trained as a stonemason, not a conventional job in the forward-thrusting United States. He moved to the UK with his British wife, presumably in part because there would be more stonemason's jobs around. He then quit his day job, however, because he had what he thought was a hit idea to create an eBay-style online marketplace for building jobs.

Some may question why an American citizen like Ryan would not take his idea to his homeland, where places like Silicon Valley are hungry for alternative digital business plans. It is a common refrain among the British that they lack the 'American dream' that inspires so many entrepreneurs (and rebel entrepreneurs) in the United States. Ryan looks at this point rather differently. 'Surely it was the British who had the American dream in the first place by travelling over on the Mayflower,' he said. You cannot argue with the logic.

He also takes a different view from most when it comes to price.

Like most start-ups, Ryan has often had to act fast to keep his personal dream on track. A couple of years ago he was about to run out of cash, just as the banking crisis struck. Up until then, My Builder had allowed the plumbers, electricians and other specialists that touted their skills on its website to register and bid for work for free

– only charging them a percentage of any work they eventually won. This made sense while the business was starting out and the priority was to build a brand presence on the web. But with the risk of bankruptcy looming, the rules had to change.

Ryan decided to introduce a registration fee for all tradespeople looking for work. The problem was that no one likes to be forced to pay for something that they previously received for free. This is particularly true in the area of internet services, where the idea that everything should be free online lingers on from the 1990s dotcom bubble. In fact, many of those reared on the web may find it hardest to believe the whole premise of this chapter, having been reared in a world where the expectation is that all sorts of things you would normally buy, from music to telephone calls, can be accessed for nothing online.

Of course, nothing is free, even on the world wide web. There may be an element of any service that is provided for free, but sooner or later a business will have to find a revenue stream.

How do you get people to pay more?

The issue for Ryan and his team was a particularly thorny one because they were trying to get customers to pay for a service they had been used to getting for free. They tried to manage the process of introducing their customers to the concept of a paid service by surveying those already registered, trying to make them feel part of the process, and sending an advance warning of the final changes by e-mail. However, this did little to soften the blow and 90 per cent of My Builder's tradespeople quit the minute the site started charging them. 'It was scary,' Ryan admitted. The good news was that the company survived.

It did this because the 10 per cent of people that stayed with the website not only enabled the business to keep trading, but helped generate My Builder's first net profit. Charging also sifted out a lot of what Ryan called 'the time wasters' on the site, leaving My Builder with people who actually won business and therefore created value for the website. Money made from subscriptions enabled Ryan to market My Builder to homeowners. As a result, the number of jobs posted on My Builder rose, which in turn increased the number of tradespeople willing to pay to register. Within 10 months, My Builder increased its subscription revenue fivefold.

Although this change in strategy produced a happy ending, Ryan admitted to me that he could equally have made other changes that might not have worked so well – such as allowing paid advertising on the website. However, it could be argued that none of these would have had the additional benefits that raising prices had on Ryan's business. In many ways raising the price proved the making of My Builder.

Price is a matter of economics

The argument for raising your price is not just about value. It is about basic economics. Put simply, if you keep your prices low, it takes a lot more sales effort to turn a profit.

David Glassman, a business coach, who has advised hundreds of ambitious entrepreneurs who wish to grow faster, explained to me the case for raising prices quite well:

> Businesses should be run to generate cash. The key task is therefore to manage for margin (the higher the better) whether the operations involve tangible goods, services or intellectual property. You can maintain margins by avoiding the temptation to chase unprofitable business through price reduction. If you reduce your price by 10 per cent when the margin is 30 per cent, you will need to increase your volume by 50 per cent to generate the previous gross profit. However, if you can justify a price increase of 10 per cent, you can generate the previous gross profit even with a volume reduction of 25 per cent. That means it is possible to remain viable without the customers who cause you problems and perhaps occasion overheads that could otherwise be shed.

In other words cutting prices not only undermines your margins, it means you have to chase more customers to make the same level of profit.

The point is that new customers are both expensive and difficult to find.

To cut, or not to cut

Companies are often tempted to cut their prices in desperation when a key customer defects. Again this is a mistake. The value of your product is equal to the cost of your customers' problems rather than to your own costs reduced by a factor to cover self-limiting beliefs.

Raising your prices does not mean you ignore rising costs. This was true at John Smedley, which employs about 450 people in its factories in jobs that are relatively low paid and repetitive. These people could easily go to other local employers, such as Tesco, for a higher wage. The company also has a small but vital team of skilled employees to hand-finish its garments. These people are in short supply in rural Derbyshire.

Cutting your costs is not the same as raising your prices

Some may take the view that instead of raising your prices, you could cut your costs. However, this would be to miss the point of creating a sense of value about your brand.

Like many small-scale UK manufacturers, John Smedley found itself under increasing pressure to move production offshore. In 2003, the company did dip a toe in south-east Asia, opening facilities in China to produce 1 per cent of its garments. Drew Walker, who was then the manufacturer's managing director, estimated that he could shave £8 off of the price of his best-selling roll-neck sweater by getting the item made in China. However, production was brought back to the UK six years later, partly because of delivery delays and quality concerns – panels were being stitched on the wrong way round, the company claimed – but mainly because the Smedley family were concerned about diluting its British brand.

The company instead has invested heavily in technology to reduce its costs. Although the company still hand-finishes garments, the machinery that makes John Smedley's fine-gauge knitwear is cutting-edge computerized technology, shipped over from Japan.

Simon Carter, the eponymous cufflink maker, is another British brand selling well abroad, which has latched onto the value of high prices. Simon is a very charismatic person, who likes business, fashion and jokes. He is also a rebel entrepreneur.

I met him at his company's flagship Mayfair shop, where his dry wit and love of double entendres was in full flow. His assistant was quickly dispatched to get 'some tarts', which created ample opportunity for innuendo from Simon. When it comes to business, however, Simon is deadly serious.

Simon Carter, which now sells across the world, from Manhattan to Sydney, is no longer just about accessories. Cufflinks made up 40 per cent of turnover in 2009, down from 57 per cent 12 months earlier. Unlike John Smedley, Simon Carter has not been afraid to move most of his manufacturing offshore. Simon told me that this was not just about keeping costs down, but because he genuinely felt manufacturing for his product was done better in countries like China.

Like John Smedley, however, price is important to maintaining the cachet of the Simon Carter brand. The global recession of 2008 and 2009 hit Simon Carter hard, partly because of its strong reliance on the Japanese market, where sales dropped by 80 per cent. It was not just that people had less money in their pockets, however, according to Simon, who admitted to me that there was a limit to how many people will buy a cufflink. The problem for Simon Carter, battling against a declining market, was very different from that facing John Smedley, which if anything had too many customers.

However, in both cases price rises have proven to be at least part of the solution. For Simon Carter, although the population of potential buyers might be declining, those that do like to buy cufflinks tended to be interested in buying multiple items. As with many items that become less common, it also seemed that those willing to buy them liked the cachet of owning one and so were willing to pay more. This was what Simon Carter was testing when I met him, when he had raised the price of his most expensive cufflink by over 50 per cent in 12 months to £75. This did not all go to the bottom line as Simon also put more money into producing his top-of-the-range items. He also stressed that the price for the entry-level cufflinks was not being touched.

The example of Simon Carter is an interesting one. By charging more for the top end, you can get more revenue from those who are arguably your best customers. In the case of Simon Carter, however, where demand was under pressure, the company made a conscious decision to have a low-priced option to ensure that new customers could sample the brand if they liked.

Richard Adams-Mercer has proved himself in the world of commerce, and he thinks that price and value go hand in hand for a business owner. His company, Parcel2Go, provides door-to-door delivery using seven of the world's biggest courier groups – and aims to provide clear, simple pricing information to customers. In terms of insurance, for example, Richard felt that the existing pricing strategy of rival delivery firms was not clear enough. Most only offered cover on their premium services or limited the insurance to crude banding levels, such as £5 for coverage up to £100 and £30 for coverage up to £300. 'This one-size-fits-all [approach] works OK for distributors for large companies but not companies like ours working with the general public,' he told me.

Richard felt he could do better, especially since Parcel2Go, like other delivery companies, uses its own reserves to cover loss and damage. So he got his IT team to set up a system on the company's website that could offer a bespoke insurance quote to customers, based on a description of the item being delivered. Not everything can be insured. For instance, Parcel2Go's system will recognize a phrase such as 'computer monitor' and say that it can insure such a delicate item for loss but not for damage. However, such openness and clever use of price has won over customers, according to Richard. In the first six weeks of the service being offered, take-up of insurance cover increased 25 per cent. The business, based in the northern English town of Bolton, in 2010 turned over £50m a year, handling in excess of 100,000 transactions a month.

The difficulty in setting a pricing structure is that one strategy is rarely relevant for everyone, and paradoxes abound.

At King & Allen, which started life as a travelling tailor bringing bespoke suits to the masses, the winning strategy since the recession began has been to introduce a higher price band for its service. In 2008, its exclusive range, in which finished suits cost between £499 and £999, accounted for just 2.6 per cent of sales, while the average amount spent by King & Allen customers was £269. By 2011, however, the situation had reversed, with 88 per cent of sales coming from the exclusive range, bringing up the average amount spent to £490. While many customers are trading down, leading to former King & Allen clients returning to off-the-peg suits at Marks & Spencer, the business has more than compensated for this, with orders from former Savile Row customers seeking the same tailor-made product for less.

The irony of an affordable-suit company gaining premium customers is not lost on co-founder Adam King. 'We haven't actually put our prices up at all,' he told me. 'We've just introduced more expensive clothes.'

The fact that there are myriad choices over how to charge for products is both the joy and the curse of the modern age, according to Doug Richard, a former panellist on the BBC pitching competition *Dragons' Den* who has since moved on to teaching aspiring entrepreneurs about the subject through his business, School for Start-ups. 'There have been many many more [pricing] business models created in the last 10 years than there were in the last 100 years,' he told me. 'The worry for people is that there are pricing models they are not thinking about.'

Doug claims that social networking technologies, such as Twitter, are also making pricing models available to the tiniest start-ups that were previously the preserve of large companies. One example is the 'yield-pricing' system that those budget airlines mentioned at the top of this chapter have used successfully for decades to fill seats on their planes by varying prices according to the demand on particular flights.

Previously, this was only possible through expensive IT systems but Doug notes that Twitter has made demand management possible even for small shops, such as local bakers. 'All you need to do is to get all your customers to sign up for a Twitter account,' he explained. 'Then, as your goods come out of the oven, you can send a tweet to tell them that hot-baked doughnuts will be available until noon at a cost of £1. After 30 minutes you send another message offering the same, colder doughnuts for 10 p.'

Roger Butterworth, former chief executive of UK-based online electronics retailer Expansys, knows something about internet pricing strategies. The business built a global following by using the efficiencies of the web to sell consumer goods at prices far lower than could be found on the high street.

Roger's second venture, Zutux, is an online marketplace that enables small businesses to sell products to consumers across the world. The pricing model is simple: the factory gate price, plus the import costs, plus a margin for Zutux. 'We think that's a very compelling customer-centric model, as opposed to the "what the market will bear" model practised by many of our competitors,' he told me.

Roger added that the pricing model fits with the business model for Zutux, which is to remove the middlemen from the market. 'We aim to be the cheapest,' he said. 'In the current market, it's hard to have a different strategy.'

Pricing strategies cannot exist in a vacuum, however. As Roger explained, it is also about the quality of service offered. 'Overservicing, and therefore overcharging customers, is as bad as providing too little service,' he said. 'I think that's one of the lessons the success of the low-cost airlines shows us.'

What about cross-border trade?

The international dimension to business can complicate pricing strategies. China and India are likely to be the world's largest economies in the next decade or so. However, what is expensive to the average Chinese consumer is still peanuts to the average American.

The rise of south-east Asian economies has been a saving grace for Benoy, a London-based architectural practice behind two of the UK's most significant shopping centres during the 1980s and 1990s: Bluewater and Lakeside. The firm does as much business in Vietnam as it does in the whole of the UK, according to Graham Cartledge, its chairman. 'We are relieved to be highly committed to the emerging markets,' he told me.

Graham's strategy for entering these markets has been to get onto the speaking circuit. He puts himself forward to speak about his high-profile projects at conferences on the countries where he would like to work. This provides a double benefit, enabling Graham to market Benoy to potential customers while he learns more about his target markets. 'I took the initiative and noticed there were several conference groups putting on events about these countries,' he explained.

One of the main challenges of operating in emerging markets – which tend to be low-cost economies – is finding the right price point for services, Graham said. For Benoy this means doing the design work in the UK and outsourcing the implementation to businesses close to the emerging market clients. The drop in the value of sterling against other currencies a few years ago changed the ratio enough to justify more work being done by the London office.

Benoy has been operating in China for about 12 years, helped by an office in Hong Kong. It has been working in India for about four, but only opened its first office there, in Mumbai, a couple of years ago with about 20 staff, hired in India and trained in London. 'One danger of becoming too local too quickly is that customers think they can buy what you do from someone else nearby,' Graham told me.

'Some of our clients like to think we are an international business rather than a local business.'

Cultural sensitivity is vital when doing business in India, according to Graham. 'It is important to engage with the local community rather than imposing yourself on them. They like to think that you engage with their culture, their history, their heritage. They want the Western solution but they don't want it just churned out. They don't want a piece of London in Mumbai.'

This said, Graham emphasizes that it is a relatively straightforward process to come to understand new cultures. 'What we have generally found is that markets are different, but probably no more different than between London and Manchester,' he explained to me. But it is also important to spend time with clients. 'You have to learn their culture, eat with them, stay with them, not just assume you can fly in, deliver a service and fly out again,' Graham said.

How do you maintain high prices?

Maintaining a high price is never easy. Just ask New & Lingwood. The 142-year-old upmarket menswear retailer and official outfitters to Eton College is a mere babe compared to John Smedley. But it has dressed seven prime ministers. The company, which sells both bespoke and ready-to-wear items, only uses British manufacturers to make its shoes and clothes. Many of these have had relationships with the company dating back 90 years. It was this heritage that attracted Anthony Spitz, a charismatic South African shoe entrepreneur, who acquired the business in 1992 with the intention of building it into a global British clothing brand. The septuagenarian, who brought Bally, Gucci and Lacoste to his homeland, told me: 'I had done everything I wanted to in South Africa and I wanted to do things in the big wide world, but I wanted to do this by owning a brand.'

His English acquisition, however, had some serious problems. One of Anthony's first tasks at New & Lingwood was to close three of its five outlets and shut its factory in the Essex town of Harlow because they were unprofitable. The business also risked having its core market cut from underneath it when rival shirt makers on London's Jermyn Street, such as TM Lewin and Thomas Pink, began expanding their outlets, putting their upmarket but cheaper shirts into high streets nationwide.

Justin Sumrie, one of New & Lingwood's two minority shareholders, along with finance director Barry Cohen, saw the problems when he joined Anthony from Holland & Holland, another luxury British brand. 'A lot of people said why do I need to spend £80 on a shirt [at New & Lingwood] when I can spend £25 elsewhere?' Neither Anthony nor his younger shareholders, however, were prepared to compromise their 'Made in England' label to compete at a lower price.

When I visited the company's Jermyn Street shop, Anthony told me that his father, from whom he inherited his retailing nous, taught him to stick with good suppliers for as long as possible. 'Become important to them and they become important to you,' Anthony said. So instead of making its shirts, shoes, pyjamas and dressing gowns more cheaply abroad, New & Lingwood's owners sought new sales by adapting the school kit they had previously sold to Britain's educational elite for an affluent adult market. For instance, its Eton branch stocked 144 variations of striped sock, catering for the myriad sports clubs and societies at Eton. By making them in merino wool, rather than the sterner fibres that English public school pupils are forced to wear, New & Lingwood created a new market for the socks as casual wear for men.

Anthony and Justin tweaked other Eton lines, including rowing caps, house scarves and boating blazers, which proved to be particularly fashionable in an era when Ralph Lauren and other world-famous designers have copied British tailoring for their globally adored preppy looks. They also took classic shoe designs such as penny loafers and produced them in bright pastel-coloured suede rather than the conventional black leather, again to appeal to young, upwardly mobile customers. These products helped create a new category of well-heeled 30- or 40-something customers for New & Lingwood in addition to its establishment and foreign clientele. This new customer group, which did not exist 10 years previously, quickly grew to account for a third of all sales.

Anthony also spent money to refresh New & Lingwood's flagship Jermyn Street shop. However, this had to be done subtly to avoid alienating long-standing establishment customers such as the late Sir James Goldsmith, the British entrepreneur who would buy 48 night shirts during a single visit and have them sent to his homes in New York and the Caribbean, Anthony told me. Simple measures, such as removing the 'awful' 30-year-old red carpet and repairing the parquet flooring, helped increase sales by 12 per cent year on year by attracting new customers to the shop, according to Justin.

New shopfloor staff were also employed, so that the average age of New & Lingwood employees dropped from the mid-50s to the late-30s. 'The old lags, who were great and had lots of experience, were relatively stuck in their ways,' Justin told me. 'Changing the age profile of the staff has meant that they have been able to give a fresh approach to the business and to the people who come through the door.'

Such alterations come at a price. Pre-tax profit more than halved from £57,000 to £21,000 during the year when the changes were made. However, the sales lift gave the new owners of New & Lingwood the confidence to push ahead with their long-standing plans for international expansion, looking at opening shops in New York.

Warning: you can raise prices too much

Of course it is possible to charge too much for a product. Anyone who has tried to travel around London by black taxi will be more than aware of this. Charming as this form of travel can be, most Londoners shun it because the fare per mile has been pushed up so high. Black cab drivers, who are themselves one-person businesses, and therefore technically entrepreneurs, complain that demand for the product is falling so they need a high price to maintain a viable livelihood. They can also hide behind the fact that black cab fares are highly regulated and controlled by the elected mayor of London. However, it can be argued that price rises for black cabs have gone beyond creating an air of luxury to destroying the market itself.

There may be entrepreneurs behind the wheel on your trip around town, but they may not be rebel entrepreneurs. In April 2010, the cost of an average daytime taxi ride in London rose by 2.7 per cent to £10.67. No doubt the cockney cabbies pointed to the fact that the cost of fuel had risen by 12 per cent in the previous 12 months. Most passengers, on the other hand, would point out that the average UK salary had risen by just 2 per cent. It seems that in this case customers really are voting with their feet. One only has to look at the long queues of black cabs outside Victoria Station in London's West End for proof of what seems suspiciously like a failing monopoly operator.

Being low cost does not mean you cannot raise your prices

Some assume that because their business was created on the premise of being a cheap alternative, they cannot raise their prices. This is not true.

To illustrate this, I'll return to a rebel entrepreneur talked about previously in this book – Jamie Murray Wells. Just to recap, he created his business, Glasses Direct, with a clever business model that allowed him to undercut the industry he was in by focusing on selling spectacles to those that needed them instead of creating a chain of opticians where he would need to spend money giving eye tests. Jamie's genius breakthrough meant that he could charge a tenth of the price high-street opticians charged and still make a profit.

I visited Glasses Direct in 2010 with Saul Klein of Index Ventures, which had become one of the key outside investors in the business.

By then its early years in Malmesbury had long gone. Jamie had become chairman, leaving day-to-day running to chief executive Kevin Cornils, and the company had moved to its smart new head-quarters in the heart of London's West End.

I was allowed to sit in on a board meeting, during which the subject of the barbecue challenge was raised. It seemed to spark a fair degree of excitement around the table, so I asked Saul about it afterwards. He explained, as we strolled past the hordes of shoppers on Regent Street, that it was all about Glasses Direct's pricing structure. You see, when Jamie first started Glasses Direct, he was able to charge £15 for a pair of spectacles that would cost someone £150 from a traditional optician. The thing was, Saul explained, he did not need to be so generous to still have a successful business. So he started raising his prices.

By the time Index had come on board, Glasses Direct's average price for a pair of spectacles had risen to £35, but in the following few years Saul and the board had got this up to £98. People still wanted to buy from Glasses Direct, but the company was able to make more money out of them. Even if this put some off buying from the company, the extra revenue more than made up for this.

Saul admitted that it was this kind of thing he usually looked at with companies his firm had just invested in. He had put the barbecue out there as a reward. If the Glasses Direct team could get the average price of their spectacles up to £120, they would start lighting the charcoal and have a well-deserved party.

'We have done the hard work, we have got people to come to the website,' Saul explained. 'Now we are seeing how much they will pay.' If Glasses Direct customers paid £120 for their spectacles, they would still be getting their lenses at 20 per cent less than the price they would have to pay on the high street. However, at this price Glasses Direct would be a much stronger business.

'People always look at how much money they make,' Saul said to me as we strolled past the high-street shoppers. 'They don't look at how much money they don't make.'

Being the best is always better than being cheapest

One solution to the difficult question of finding the right price is to consider charging different prices at different times. Responding to changes in demand is OK. Airlines, cinemas and ice-cream sellers do it. A community café could do it to profit from affluent workers with limited time at lunchtimes, allowing others who are time-rich and cash-poor to eat more cheaply mid-afternoon.

Ultimately, however, the mantra of a true rebel entrepreneur should be to compete on quality, not price. 'Better, not cheaper' is a more sustainable mantra than 'more for less'.

Price your products and services so you can offer discounts by working out three prices. The top 'dream price' represents the real value of your input. The middle price should represent a good profit margin. The bottom price is the one you should never go below. Start by asking your dream price and only negotiate down for bulk orders, payment up front and so on. There are 101 reasons why someone does or doesn't buy a product or service, and price is just one of them.

Don't get hung up on pricing but, if you think it's particularly important for your offering and customer group, test that theory before you go too far with a bit of research. It seems that too often people fail to put up their prices because they fear that they will price themselves out of their market. Such timidity is not worthy of a successful rebel entrepreneur. In fact, as Simon Carter showed, raising your prices may be a way to squeeze more value out of your existing customers in times when general demand for your product is declining.

The conclusion

The key point about this chapter is the need to think of price as a branding message about the quality of your product or service, not just the means of covering your costs.

The biggest danger to your business ultimately is not the loss of sales, but the fact that you might run out of cash to pay your bills. Raising your prices may well be the way to avoid this.

Raising your prices may also be a smart thing to do in times of economic downturn as a way of showing that your product has value and is therefore worth paying a little more for.

The problem with trying to compete on price is that there can only be one business with the lowest prices, and the cost of achieving this is often high.

Chapter Five
Don't get hung up on the business plan

One of the key messages of this book is that successful entrepreneurship is about realizing that life does not always work out the way that you planned it, no matter how much effort and skill you have put into that process. This does not necessarily mean that your business fails – although I will talk about that issue in the final chapter. It is about the way that most of what we consider the greatest business ideas are in fact an adaptation of an original idea, or perhaps even a completely new concept hit upon by the founding team when their first approach was not working out.

The problem is that in business you need to make plans. These then become a document – the business plan – that helps you and your backers understand just exactly what it is that you are trying to do. The problem then becomes knowing when to adapt or even tear up the script and start with something new.

As Robert Burns said in his poem *To a Mouse*:

The best laid schemes o' mice an' men
    Gang aft agley.

Planning is important. Attention to detail is also vital. But if you do not have the flexibility to admit that you are wrong and change your plans accordingly, you may well miss out on the opportunity to build a bigger, better business. The point of this chapter is to talk about how any business idea has to be fluid in nature, able to change and adapt to take advantage of what may well be a bigger proposition than the founder envisaged. The reason why rebel entrepreneurs succeed is that they managed to move on and change what they were doing at precisely the right time. Sometimes, as we shall discover, this is more by luck than design, but it is often essential if you are to turn a good idea into a great one.

There is a tension between the two great entrepreneurial traits: attention to detail and the ability to think outside conventional understanding. Those who have combined these have done some amazing things, as we shall see in this chapter, but it is a journey fraught with problems.

That is what this chapter is all about.

The only constant in (business) life is change

The business plan is often placed as the cornerstone of any decent start-up, involving careful research and preparation.

This is all well and good. The danger, however, is that a company's founders turn this document from a useful guide into a sacred text, from which they refuse to swerve. Swerving, or pivoting, is actually the secret to some of the fastest-growing companies. But more of those concepts later in this chapter. For now let us look at the idea that it is good practice not to get too hung up on a business plan.

Why is this so?

Firstly, as has been noted earlier in this book, fast business growth is very much the exception rather than the norm in economic life. The OECD, the international body that offers advice to governments on economic and social issues, calculated that fast-growing companies, commonly referred to these days as gazelle businesses, make up less than 1 per cent of the total business population in terms of employment and less than 2 per cent in terms of sales. These gazelles are therefore very rare beasts indeed.

The exact moment when a company will enter a period of fast growth is also very difficult to predict. In 2005, Charlene Nicholls Nixon, a professor of entrepreneurship at the IESE Business School at the University of Navarra in the United States, studied details of the Fortune 500, a ranking of the fastest-growing US-based companies according to their annual sales growth in the previous five years. Over a 22-year period, Professor Nixon found that only 69 businesses made it on to the list more than once. It is a sobering thought that even if you have a fast-growing business today, that is no guarantee of future success.

Such data illustrates the, in some senses, random nature of fast growth; it suggests that even if you are growing fast today, that is no guarantee that you will grow fast tomorrow. Indeed if you do it will probably be because you have changed in some way.

The good news is that it may just take one big change to strike entrepreneurial gold.

Ryanair as an example of a company that changed

Take Ryanair. Today it is the second largest carrier in Europe in terms of passenger numbers and the largest in the world in terms of international passenger numbers. But this might never have happened had it not been for some crucial adjustments to the core business model.

The company was founded by Irish businessmen Tony Ryan, Christy Ryan and Liam Lonergan in 1985 with a fairly modest aim: to fly between Waterford, in the Republic of Ireland, and London. The original aim was to provide something better than the existing carriers, British Airways and Aer Lingus, at the time both government-owned airlines. The problem was that Ryanair was trying to undercut its rivals while matching them on the fancy extras that made plane travel so expensive in the first place.

It soon became obvious that the original business plan was not working as well as had been first hoped. The owners of Ryanair tried adding another route to their schedule, from Dublin to London, but this made little difference. Although the airline was adding passengers, it was suffering losses, and the founders decided that they needed to restructure.

It was time to make some changes. The first fundamentally important change was to hire Michael O'Leary, an accountancy graduate who had been Tony Ryan's personal tax adviser. As well as being good with numbers, Mr O'Leary had a strong competitive instinct.

His first move proved his credentials as a rebel entrepreneur: he chose to imitate someone else's business model. In particular, he focused on Southwest Airlines, a pioneer of the model of low-fare, no-frills air travel in the United States. (I would say in the world, but no-frills air travel had been tried before, by the UK's Sir Freddie Laker. However, Sir Freddie was unable to make his business model work for several reasons, not least of which was that he chose to do it on long-distance routes where he was undercut by rivals.)

Mr O'Leary travelled to the United States to study the business model created by Herb Kelleher, founder of Southwest Airlines. Mr Kelleher had grown Southwest into one of the most consistently profitable carriers in the world by being very good at what he did, which meant slicing away unnecessary costs in the air travel business. His advice to Mr O'Leary was simple: fly only one model of plane to minimize engineering costs; drive down costs every year and turn round the aircraft at the terminals as quickly as you can.

Imitate, don't innovate (reprised)

Mr O'Leary returned to Ireland determined to ape his American mentor. We have already seen in Chapter 2 of this book the value of copying another company's successful business model. That is exactly what Mr O'Leary did.

He took Mr Kelleher's advice and bought just one model of aircraft for Ryanair, a basic version of the Boeing 737. This tweak to the business model meant that it was easier and cheaper to train maintenance staff, and that Ryanair only needed to keep one list of spare parts.

The second change was to greatly increase the number of destinations, while all the time choosing to fly point-to-point. You could add to this a third change in that Mr O'Leary decided to fly to the less well-used airports that were close but maybe not the closest to their destination cities. This led to some jokes about Ryanair never getting to the places that it claimed it was flying to, but the use of second-tier airports kept costs down.

After a successful flotation on the Dublin Stock Exchange and the New York Nasdaq in 1997, Ryanair had the cash to achieve all of these goals. It launched services to Stockholm, Oslo, Paris-Beauvais and Charleroi, a town near Brussels. It followed this with a $2 bn order for 45 new Boeing 737-800 series aircraft.

Mr O'Leary made another key change to the Ryanair business model by betting that the internet would be the main way people would buy their travel tickets in future instead of the phone. At the time that Ryanair launched its website, in 2000, this was still not a certainty. The dotcom bubble had burst and there was great cynicism about the medium's potential after so many failed business plans. However, it quickly started to work for Ryanair. Online sales also meant that Ryanair no longer needed to shell out for a call centre or pay travel agents; thus the Ryanair website saved on marketing costs. By 2003, more than 90 per cent of Ryanair's bookings were made online, even better than Southwest's 59 per cent.

Mr O'Leary has attracted a fair amount of controversy over the years, most notably when he said he was going to charge people to use his plane's toilets during flights, which caused a particular stink. However, he has never forgotten the lessons of Southwest, particularly the need to constantly cut out costs. The tweaks and adjustments to Ryanair's way of operating have also enabled Mr O'Leary to surpass even the achievements of the company that guided him. For the full year 2007, Ryanair reported a profit of €435 m on revenues of €2.2 bn, or 20 per cent of sales, an almost unbeatable profit margin for the airline industry. Southwest meanwhile reported a pre-tax profit of $1.05 bn or 10.6 per cent of sales on $9.8 bn in revenues.

Ryanair was helped along the way by other factors, not least the opening up of European air travel to greater competition by the EU. But there is little doubt that the company would not be the powerhouse it is today without Mr O'Leary's significant leadership, and the changes he has made to the way the company operates.

There is no shame in starting all over again

The one constant in life, as the cliché goes, is change. And yet, how many times do you hear about the need for a properly thought out business plan in order to have a successful business? It is perhaps not surprising that the people most often asking for these documents are bank managers and business studies professors, two professions not known for their entrepreneurial flair.

This is not to say that you do not need to prepare a detailed plan or spend a considerable amount of time on research. The point is to realize that your original assumptions may well have to be adjusted as your business begins trading and you see how customers react to what you offer. It is often only in doing so that you see how to do things better.

If you do not spot the need to make alterations and adjust your plan accordingly, you may not achieve anywhere near the growth you planned or intended to achieve.

Testing, testing

It is also important to test your theories regularly. Probably the best way to do this is to start small, and be prepared to see your original assumptions shot down by experience. This can become a constant process of changing and adapting.

Sometimes, however, it is the whole idea that needs to be screwed up and thrown in the rubbish bin in order to start again. This was the case for Dominic Lake, a rebel entrepreneur I was introduced to a few years ago.

Dominic's first passion was industrial design, which he studied to degree level at Central Saint Martins college in London. He was introduced to the world of entrepreneurship soon after graduating, when he was hired to spot promising companies by a private equity investor.

'What I rapidly realized was that I loved all of the businesses I saw,' he told me over a coffee in Canary Wharf. 'I didn't have a framework to assess those businesses as I didn't have an experience of running an entrepreneurial business.' To help him get some formal understanding of what to look out for, Dominic's employer enrolled him on the executive MBA course at London Business School. 'There was all this corporate finance stuff. It was really very interesting but I didn't get a lot of it,' Dominic told me. He added that what he learnt about entrepreneurship was that it was really about common sense and understanding the action and reaction you get from doing certain things.

Getting a little academic understanding was not such a bad idea for someone who by then realized that his long-term goal was to start a company of his own, and London Business School in particular was a good venue for an aspiring rebel entrepreneur like Dominic. It has a long tradition of nurturing entrepreneurial talent, whether through its MBA course or its entrepreneurs' summer school. Its students also invite experienced entrepreneurs to the campus, near Regent's Park, to give evening lectures about the lessons they have learnt in building businesses. Former alumni include successful entrepreneurs such as Tony Wheeler, founder of the Lonely Planet guides.

Dominic saw the opportunity to pick up some skills on the MBA course that would enable him to be a better entrepreneur. But first he needed an idea that worked. In the last weeks of study at the Business

School, one of the focuses for the students was their own business plan. This was when Dominic started trying to form the ideal business for him.

For a long time, he had been a car enthusiast, so his first idea was to smarten up the vehicle-repair industry with a chain of upmarket garages. He was encouraged by the fact that a number of friends had also opened their own car-repair shops.

This plan, however, like the badly built mass-manufacture British cars of the 1970s and 1980s, stalled before it had ever really got started. After conducting many hours of research, Dominic could not get away from the concern that the whole business was reliant on the funding of insurance companies. This meant that everything was about the price a job could be done for rather than the quality of the experience.

The problem, Dominic realized, was that the repair shops bought labour at £19 an hour, which didn't leave much margin once the owner of the garage paid all the large operational costs. What had happened, it transpired, was that the existing repair shops, in order to make any margin at all, were overestimating the amount of time it took to do the job, as Dominic explained. 'Somehow that business seemed to function, but it was not one I wanted to be involved in.'

Rather than tweak the idea, Dominic moved on from this first business plan and embarked on something completely different. He had been introduced to Patrick Clayton-Malone, who was married to an old friend of his and had recently moved to the same part of London as Dominic. The two had lunch together and hit it off immediately. They found they had a lot in common, not least because Patrick was also looking to start a venture, so they decided to form an alliance.

First off, Dominic helped Patrick with a plan to open a boutique hotel in Bath. However, this idea proved problematic in practice. What they both wanted was a business that they could grow to some-thing of considerable scale. But once they got into the hotel idea, they found that would be difficult with the approach they had taken. The combination of the property side of the business and the food side made the business model too complex, Dominic explained to me.

Instead of trying to pursue something they both did not feel completely confident about, the pair decided to switch to restaurants, figuring that this would be a simpler proposition. Again, they showed that they were not afraid to turn an idea down if it was not working.

They also saw an opportunity to bring their individual talents to bear on the venture, differentiating it in what is a crowded market. Both Patrick and Dominic had a passion for food and design. They then met another foodie in the form of chef Cass Titcombe. Together, they came up with a plan for a chain of restaurants across the UK that would serve classic British dishes. Of course, British-themed restaurants had become a well-trodden path for many restaurateurs. Dominic, Patrick and Cass brought a new twist by making it all about modern Britain, using new furniture made by British manufacturers and cooking with locally sourced ingredients.

The timing was also good. When they started their chain, in the late 1990s, British cooking was starting to emerge on the world stage as something to be reckoned with rather than joked about. British chefs, such as Heston Blumenthal and Jamie Oliver, were making a name for themselves in the media, both in the UK and abroad. But no one had yet produced a chain of reasonably priced restaurants specifically aimed at those looking for good-quality British cooking.

Dominic and Patrick saw their chance. Their first restaurant of the chain, which they called Canteen, opened its doors in October 2005 with an outlet in the newly redecorated Spitalfields, a former Victorian fruit and vegetable market in the City of London. It quickly grew to a chain of four sites, including the Canary Wharf restaurant, which got a prime location within the complex's central tall tower.

They also wanted to use their passion for design so they extended the 'Made in Britain' theme to the interior design of their new restaurants. The Canary Wharf venue where I met Dominic was the company's second outlet and provided a classic example of the founder's approach. Even the oak tables we ate our dinner at were locally sourced, made by a company in Chiswick, west London.

Dominic had a successful business idea, albeit at his third attempt. He just needed to plan the detail.

Once the business plan works, write it down

Before the business could get started, Dominic still had to sit down and prepare a business plan for the Canteen concept. He did this with a five-year set of targets that he and his co-founders came up with over the course of 18 months.

When I met Dominic in 2010, he was able to boast about the accuracy of the predictions he had made five years earlier, such as the growth in revenue. The point was not, however, that he had made a business plan for the idea that worked. It was that he was prepared to ditch the business plans for the previous ideas when they showed they did not stack up.

Dominic's story is a common one, according to John Mullins, an associate professor at London Business School, who with Randy Komisar co-wrote the book *Getting to Plan B* about just this issue. Arguably, Professor Mullins should have renamed his tome *Getting to Plan C*, as he admits that it is often only on the third time of trying that successful entrepreneurs get it right. Many do not even get this far. 'The track record of entrepreneurial ventures in general is that the vast majority fail,' Professor Mullins wrote. 'For Max Levchin [founder of online payments service PayPal], it was plan G that worked.'

The problem with sticking to that first plan, no matter how good it seems on paper, is that the harsh realities of life are too often likely to derail it. The reason is uncertainty.

I have spoken to Professor Mullins about this issue now several times. One of the pearls of wisdom he has offered to me is this: 'There are things that you know you don't know but there are also things you don't know that you don't know – the unknown unknowns.' Successful entrepreneurs are not those who push their original ideas at all costs but those who work out which of their original assumptions are wrong and stop pursuing them, according to Professor Mullins.

> Your key job is to learn quickly which parts of your business plan are not right and change them without wasting a lot of your money and that of your investors.

Looking outside your business to what others have done is also critical to success, according to Professor Mullins. 'Too many entrepreneurs feel that they have found a new paradigm. There is an awful lot of learning to be done by looking around.'

Professor Mullins is an advocate of the approach taken by Ryanair, of blatantly copying another person's business model but then being even sharper at delivering on that model. 'The answer is not to get so wrapped up in your own idea, but to learn from others,' he told me. 'There is really nothing radically different under the sun. Someone has done something like what you have done before.'

The final point, according to Professor Mullins, is to get the main structural elements of the business model right. These are: revenue, gross margin, opportunity capital, working capital and the investment model.

The problem for founders is that reality is seldom as simple as the academic theory would have us believe. Bob Rae moved through several business models after founding a company with former colleague Bob Archibold in August 1982. Archibold Rae Consultants (ARC) started life as a Berkshire-based headhunting operation for multinationals setting up in the UK. However, within a couple of years, it had added an executive relocation business, having spotted that there was a parallel demand for help in moving people once they had accepted a job. By 1989, ARC was the largest relocation business in the UK, with more than 200 corporate clients, including Glaxo, Pfizer, Bass and Mobil Oil. Bob had also set up a training business in

Manchester, an IT recruitment company in London and a corporate consultancy in Munich to complement his initial ventures.

Then, the 1989 recession struck, forcing property prices down and unemployment up. ARC Group's revenues were halved almost overnight and the business, which employed about 140 people at the time, was unable to cut costs quickly enough. 'We worked out that, if we fired everyone, we would still be making a loss,' Bob told me.

A new business plan was no longer a choice but a necessity. Bob closed the IT recruitment business and the Munich consultancy and sold the training company. But he also moved into new markets – setting up an information business that provided companies looking at relocating their operations with details of potential locations, and another venture selling repossessed properties for banks and building societies. This latter company, ARC Real Estate, was changed again to a business that bought properties from people who needed to relocate for work so that they could finance a home near their new workplace.

In 2010, the newly adjusted company produced a £4 m operating profit on £25 m turnover, Bob's best year since he set up on his own almost 30 years previously.

To Bob, adapting his business model was a matter of survival. It is also about diversifying to spread the risk. 'As an entrepreneur you are always defensive,' he told me. 'Most of the time I think, "If I don't earn another penny, how long can I survive?"'

The concept of the pivot

The need to tweak business plans to build an even better business model has produced a new phrase in the Californian start-up Mecca, Silicon Valley. A few years ago people in the Palo Alto community started talking about 'making a pivot', a term taken from basketball, where players turn themselves in different directions, without moving their feet, in order to find the best person to pass the ball to.

Mark Suster, general partner at Los Angeles-based venture capital firm GRP Partners, told me that the ability to pivot is one of the key characteristics of a successful entrepreneur. 'Every entrepreneur starts with an idea that they believe makes sense,' he said. 'But then your customers start using your products, your competitors come out with new offerings and your partners decide to launch a similar product rather than working with you. You're forced to pivot on a regular basis.'

He notes that almost all software start-ups in Silicon Valley now build their businesses on this basis. Google and PayPal, two of the Valley's biggest recent success stories, both pivoted, he noted. 'Minimum viable product is the mantra of the Valley. Rather than launching a bloated product that the market does not want, you look and learn.' Often, a pivot is necessary because the market does not know what it wants. This makes it all the more important to get something out there, then refine it using feedback from customers and focus groups.

It was Australian entrepreneur Alicia Navarro who introduced me to the concept of pivoting, during a night out with a group of London-based business founders in a pub near Baker Street. She had set up her company, Skimlinks, four years previously, believing at the time she had a great business plan. Alicia had spotted that people often have better experiences when they make group decisions about key activities, such as planning a holiday or buying a sofa. So she set up her company as a social decision-making website.

The initial business plan for Skimlinks was not quite right, however. The technology was being built by a team of developers in Romania, while Alicia was based at the time in Sydney, Australia, trying to nurture her start-up at the same time as holding down a full-time job. Rather than give in and try a completely new business, however, Alicia went about altering some of the elements of her original idea. This was her first pivot.

Alicia made multiple pivots with her business. First, there was the personal: she relocated herself from Sydney to London's Shoreditch to be close to Europe's main internet business cluster.

London's East End has been transformed in recent years from a rather run-down district on the edge of the city's financial centre, best known for strip joints and badly built council flats, into a Mecca for wannabe Mark Zuckerbergs. Hundreds of tech start-ups now operate out of the streets between Shoreditch High Street and Old Street, known as Silicon Roundabout.

Once ensconced in the London scene, Alicia marketed her business to online publishers who wanted to use it on their websites as a 'white-label service', whereby the company provided its service under someone else's brand. She won customers, got friends to invest and secured a bank loan, allowing her to employ four people. But it was still a fairly hand-to-mouth existence. 'Every month, it was a nightmare working out how I would do payroll, but I always found a way, and kept it going,' she admitted to me.

When the global recession hit in September 2008, however, Alicia found herself facing the prospect of bankruptcy. It was then that she made what she has since realized was one of her smartest pivots to date. 'As I was pitching my company to potential clients and investors, it struck me that what everyone was interested in wasn't my fabulous website, but this techie back-end solution,' she recalled. She realized that she needed to change what she was selling to give Skimlinks the lift she desired.

Alicia made her pivot at 10 pm one Friday night, when she cold-called a large electronics forum website and offered them her technology. They said yes, and Alicia promised to get something to them within a fortnight. It meant changing a model that Alicia and her team had worked on for two years, but she managed to win them all over to the idea.

Over the next two weeks, she went out and sold the concept to some large UK content networks. 'My team converted what we had built into something other publishers could use,' Alicia told me. A month after relaunching the business, in December 2008, she had an agreement with an equity investor. A year later, the business was breaking even and serving over 500,000 websites worldwide, working with 8,000 retailers as well as winning dozens of awards for innovation.

The company had pivoted in London, but in 2010 Alicia made another change, moving herself to San Francisco to be part of the Silicon Valley itself. Skimlinks today is, in many ways, entirely different from the original plan, but Alicia acknowledges that pivoting made the difference between success and failure. 'That late-night decision to pivot is what saved us,' she told me.

Another successful pivoter is Richard Moross, founder of Moo.com, whom I first talked about in Chapter 3. Unlike Alicia, Richard decided to remain in the Silicon Roundabout area and is now a central figure in that fast-growing start-up community.

Moo.com started life in 2004 as a social networking website, with the twist that users could send their details to one another on real business cards. 'It was basically Facebook with cards,' Richard told me. However, the business was not taking off in the way Richard had intended. 'People loved the little cards, but they didn't want to join another social network.'

The first pivot was to change the name. For some reason, which even he wonders at now, Richard had initially called his company Pleasure Cards. 'Every time I mention it, a bit of me dies,' he said to me. His first main pivot in the business plan – something Richard describes as 'more of a pirouette' – was to drop the social networking site element. Instead, Moo.com started working with established social networks, such as Flickr, the US-based picture website, giving users the ability to put downloaded images onto paper business cards. Richard's other pivot was to extend Moo.com's portfolio of cards beyond its original mini-cards to more conventional shapes.

Not all these ideas worked (folded notecards for example), necessitating another pivot back to the core business proposition.

Pivoting is all very well, but a good entrepreneur focuses on what he or she is good at.

In Moo.com's case, Richard said that he could have gone for the consumer market by selling lots of different greetings cards, but pulled back from this because it would have required a very different business model. 'I guess we have learnt a lot about what works and what doesn't work,' he explained to me. 'When I started out, I was very stubborn. I had something I wanted to do and I wanted to do it my way. I am still stubborn on some things but I am also very flexible on what customers want.'

While pivoting is important to almost every highly successful enterprise, it can take different forms, according to Mark Suster at GRP Partners. 'Most serial entrepreneurs who are working on an early-stage concept know that whatever they're working on in year one is likely to be dramatically different from what they're doing in year five,' he said. 'That might mean a totally different business or it might just be a totally different business model.'

Often pivoting is a case of making minor changes, such as updating a software service with new releases of a technology that does things customers like better. 'For me, it starts with customer feedback, and that usually ends up creating minor pivots,' Mark said. 'The best entrepreneurs get market feedback regularly and change their approach based on the latest information. The best entrepreneurs seek advice from everybody they need, learn lessons and make minor adjustments on a monthly basis.'

What Mark describes as 'major' pivots are those instances when a business owner notices fundamental changes in a market and adjusts to them 'on a dime'. An example of this is Facebook, which in 2011 made big changes to its business model, inspired by the stream of messages seen on rival social networking website Twitter, Mark noted. 'Facebook saw that Twitter was getting massive adoption and realized what people really cared about was the stream. What they did was obliterate their home page and in a single day they refocused the entire orientation of the company on the stream.'

That, Mark said, is one of the main reasons why Facebook founder Mark Zuckerberg has been so successful.

Pivoting once is never enough

Twitter itself is a triumph of pivoting. The business, which in 2011 was valued at more than $5 bn, started life as the offshoot of a web start-up called Odeo. The original plan of Odeo's founders had been to create a platform on the internet for people to create podcasts. The trouble was that Apple then decided to add a podcasting platform to its wildly successful iTunes music download service. It looked like game over for Odeo.

In desperation, the company started scratching around for new ideas. One way it did this was to organize brainstorming sessions in down periods during the working day. It also encouraged the company's IT developers to take a day off to work on new ideas in a sort of contest called a 'hackathon'.

It was at one lunchtime brainstorming session that the idea for Twitter was suggested by Odeo employee Jack Dorsey. The team happened to be in a children's playground. Sitting at the top of the slide, Mr Dorsey suggested a business plan for an SMS (or text) service to communicate privately with people in a small group. A 140-character limit was placed on it because 160 characters was the maximum allowed for a single text message by most US carriers at the time, and Twitter's founders wanted to leave enough space for people to write their names.

There is some disagreement about what happened next, but the generally accepted story is that Odeo was rescued from itself by the inventors of Twitter. In October 2006, Biz Stone, Evan Williams, Jack Dorsey and other members of Odeo formed Obvious Corporation and acquired Odeo and all of its assets, including Twitter.com, from the investors and shareholders. Twitter was spun off into its own company in April 2007.

The tipping point for Twitter came later that year at the South by Southwest festival, a film and music festival held in Austin, Texas. Twitter's staff placed two 60-inch television screens in the hallways of the venue, enabling conference goers to keep tabs on each other via the messages posted. During the event, Twitter usage increased from 20,000 to 60,000 tweets a day. Four years later the number of customers had grown to more than 200 million active users, generating 65 million tweets a day and handling over 800,000 search queries per day.

All this growth came from one suggestion on the top of a slide in a California playground by a worker trying to save a sinking company.

'If you don't spot these major things happening in your market, then the life of your company will be very short,' Mark Suster said. He claimed that he looks for entrepreneurs who have 'a mindset to pivot' when he is making investments. This means that he spends a long time getting to know the founder before committing to putting money into the business. 'I tend to invest in people who I have got to know over a 6-, 9- or 12-month period,' he told me. 'I want to judge how they pivot.'

Mark added that he might not invest in individuals until they are on their third or fourth business idea, as their ability to do this shows him that they have the potential to pivot a business model.

So is it wise to make a business plan if all you are going to do is change it?

It seems fair to say that a lot of the argument for having a business plan comes from those providing the cash for new ventures. Business plans are needed to convince banks to lend money and to attract other investors.

The principle of writing everything down beforehand is beginning to be questioned, however. Ian Sanders, co-author of *Unplan Your Business*, is perhaps unsurprisingly in the no camp. 'There are plans that take months – years even – and plans that are a bit more rapid than that,' he told me. The business plan for Hotmail was written overnight by one of the founders, Sabeer Bhatia, Ian noted. 'It was enough to secure finances to hire programmers to create the webmail service that was later sold to Microsoft for $400 m.' Others are not quite so quick, with management teams, analysts and advisers spending months producing financial projections, pie charts and graphs.

'If you don't require investment to get your idea up and running, then maybe you only need the time it takes to drink a cup of hot tea to get your plan down on paper,' Ian told me.

One of those who believes that every business needs a business plan is Paul Marson-Smith, managing partner at Gresham Private Equity. (Those in private equity are another group, alongside bankers and academics, for whom business plans can be sacred.) 'You wouldn't drive a car without a dashboard,' he told me. 'Sure, there are assumptions in there and, sure, they are not accurate, but they are the best guess at the time.'

Even he admits, however, that smart entrepreneurs should build contingency into whatever they write down because not everything goes to plan. 'The business plan is a piece of engineering, and as with any structure there needs to be a degree of tolerance to the business plan,' Paul told me. 'It needs to be a live document that gets discussed in board meetings. The people running the business should be clear that the goals they are being set are aligned with the business plan and the plan is always aligned with the shareholder strategy.'

Another pair of entrepreneurs who had to make dramatic changes to their business plans were the owners of Urang. When Steve Bushell and Paul Cleaver bought into the business (pronounced 'you rang') in 2000, it was a concierge service, securing tables at London's finest restaurants or tickets for the latest West End theatre productions for time-poor City professionals. Neither Steve, whose background was in operations at UK technology companies, nor Paul, a former M&A specialist at investment bank Rothschilds, had any experience in this sector. However, both believed they could make it work.

At the time, when the 1990s dotcom bubble was still being inflated by hype about the power of the web, this made eminent sense: banks and professional service firms were signing company-wide deals for such services so that they could offer them as perks to retain key staff. In Urang, Steve and Paul saw an opportunity to buy into an established business, which had already built a small operation but was in desperate need of a cash injection. For only £5,000 each, they were able to acquire a two-thirds stake and run the business along-side its founder.

The problem was that although Urang was adding customers – eventually generating a regular income from 400 individual member-ships – it never managed to win a big corporate contract. When the dotcom bubble burst in 2001, banks and legal firms switched from hiring to firing – and the owners of Urang realized that they needed a plan B.

An opportunity presented itself from customer inquiries. One of the most popular requests from Urang members was for good trades-people to undertake home improvements and repairs. Paul and Steve began to wonder whether focusing on this kind of work, which in any case generated higher margins than restaurant bookings and theatre tickets, would actually be better than persisting with trying to make the concierge operation work.

Another idea was to set up a property management services division. Both Paul and Steve were living in buildings that paid annual service charges to property management companies for the maintenance of shared living spaces, and both of them felt the job could be done better. When the contracts on their buildings came up for renewal, Steve pitched himself to manage Paul's property and vice versa. Both men's bids succeeded, and Urang tied another string to its bow.

'The key is to be open to new ideas, rather than saying: "We set this business up to do X and we will only do X,"' Steve said. 'The opportunity is always there.'

The market ended up deciding whether Steve and Paul should scale down the concierge operation. Of the handful of concierge businesses that were operating when Urang began trading, only one now survives. Instead of making a dramatic break, however, Urang's concierge busi-ness was gradually phased out as the company built up its new home improvement, office refurbishment and property management arms. By 2007, the company had sales of £6 m and had grown from three people in a cramped room to a staff of about 25 people in a serviced office space.

One of the reasons Urang was able to change its focus so dramatically was that it never sought funding from external investors who demanded that they 'stick to the knitting', as Steve puts it. Bootstrapping, as I outlined in Chapter 1, has its uses.

This is not to say that the path was easy for Steve and Paul. Changing the business model did not immunize Urang from the effects of the financial crisis or the recession that followed in its wake. Sales dropped by a third in the three years after the crisis, although Steve stressed to me that profit remained stable because the business found ways to improve its margins. The business was also hit by losses from some of the original home improvement and office renovation contracts.

As a result, in 2009 Paul and Steve set up a new holding company, Urang Group, making themselves joint owners, with separate limited liability businesses responsible for each of Urang's different services. The business continues to evolve and add new elements to its operations.

Urang is now authorized by the Financial Services Authority, the UK regulatory body, to sell building insurance to the 240 properties it manages across London. When I spoke to them, Steve and Paul were also planning to open a kitchens-and-bathrooms showroom to help cross-sell Urang's home improvement services to residents in its managed properties.

Pivoting and foreign markets

One area where business owners often find they have to revise their plans is in foreign expansions.

Ten Group is the London-based international concierge business that outlasted Urang and took control of the market. It was created by Alex Cheatle, who is the brother of The Supper Club's Duncan Cheatle. He too had tried other ideas before hitting upon Ten, whose sole purpose was to enable wealthy people – who have money but no time – to get whatever they want, wherever they happen to be on the planet. Such a business, serving people who fly across the world at a moment's notice, appears to be one that can be easily exported. Wrong, according to Alex. Ten's first attempt at going global in 2000, when it opened offices in Australia and Germany, ended in disaster and the business had to retrench.

One reason it did not work was that the company had tried its international expansion before it got its business plan working properly, Alex told me. 'We were rolling out a model around the world as if it was successful, when it wasn't.' A more specific problem that made it difficult for Ten to start exporting at first was that it could not commit enough senior management time to make the expansion work. 'When you have got 95 per cent of your business in the UK and 5 per cent abroad, exporting can feel like a hobby business,' Alex told me.

Second time around, Ten was much more successful. In 2007, it opened a Hong Kong office, later adding teams in New York and San Francisco to ensure it had people on the ground at any time clients needed them. A local presence also brought all-important local knowledge in markets such as the United States.

Ten now has clients in all corners of the world. It is able to speak to them in nine different languages, including Mandarin and Russian, whatever time they choose to call with a request.

People are always critical to major changes like this. One of the key lessons Alex believed that he learnt was to put senior people in charge of new offices abroad. In the case of San Francisco, this meant having the company's head of operations move to a new continent to run the show. Fortunately, he was happy with the arrangement – not least because his long-term girlfriend was an American. Alex told me that he wouldn't have set up in the United States if he hadn't been able to appoint one of his senior team to do the job. Now that he has, his company is able to reap the rewards.

'Although we share the same language with Americans, they are not going to give a contract to a company based in London.' In this respect, though, Americans are in a minority. Ten is able to serve most of its foreign clients from London, and two-thirds of the company's 300 employees are based at its UK headquarters. 'Quite a lot of our Russian members, for instance, quite like it that we are based in London,' Alex said.

I have met Alex on several occasions over the years, and I have learnt that he sees entrepreneurship as a similar job to an artist creating something of value. Like the painter producing a masterpiece, the entrepreneur may need from time to time to wipe away or paint over what has already been done to make the final piece an exceptional work of art. Of course, the satisfaction of creating a great business is also rewarded with substantial wealth if the tweaking of the business plan is correctly accomplished. However, there is something to Alex's analogy.

Another entrepreneur who has had to make significant changes to his business model is Michael Conway, founder of The Quayside Group. When he started Quayside in 1995, the business was a clothing importer supplying leading UK high-street retailers such as Next, House of Fraser, Mothercare, C&A and Debenhams. But in spite of early success, the business was hit by a number of shocks as big customers went into receivership, withdrew from the UK market or changed their sourcing policies. 'It meant we had great difficulty growing the business,' Michael explained to me.

The big turning point came five years into the life of the company when Sir Philip Green, the British retail entrepreneur, bought BHS, another major national clothing chain, and started to source directly rather than through importers. 'It became clear that I was in a declining market segment which had high risks and low profit margins,' Michael said. 'It was like being a rabbit caught in the headlights, with 15 years' experience in a market sector that was disappearing fast.'

Michael decided to focus on internet retail and tried to find niches that Quayside could supply. He switched the company's focus away from selling to retailers and towards selling workwear and clothing for events to other businesses where there was less competition.

Again there were problems. The first website was designed by an outside agency and took 18 months to build. It was a total failure, Michael admitted. He then resolved 'to learn everything I could about websites, online marketing and search engine optimization'. Michael, like Steve Bushell and Paul Cleaver, would be the first to admit that change is not always easy – but if they had not changed, their businesses might not have survived the movements in their markets. Changing your business strategy is often necessary, but seldom easy. Sometimes, however, the best ideas come about when you have little choice.

We looked in Chapter 4 at the changes Ryan Notz made to the pricing model of his business My Builder, which, while difficult, proved to be the making of his company. Subsequently, Ryan made further adjustments to his business model, which proved just as hard to implement but equally necessary. One adjustment that caused a particular backlash, both from My Builder's board and tradespeople using the site, was Ryan's decision to prevent people from bidding for work unless they were based close to the address of the customer and skilled in the task required. The perception was that Ryan was restricting choice, although he told me that the net effect was to improve the service for My Builder's customers, as it stopped them being inundated with speculative quotes from tradespeople adopting a scattergun approach to finding work. 'You have to understand why these people are complaining,' he told me. 'You have to give these things time.'

For Dominic List at Comtact, an IT services company, strategic change has been about making more out of the existing resources in the business. Dominic and his team went through their customer lists and contacted those on whom they were losing money. They told these customers that they might be better off with one of Comtact's competitors. As a result, Comtact lost a fifth of its 200 customers, but it was able to add £150,000 to gross profit – which Dominic reinvested in more customer service, technical support and engineering staff. 'It was a leap of faith,' he explained to me, adding that he had to tell staff that the short-term pain of making the move would be worth it in terms of more happy customers in the future.

'Some staff were unsettled by the whole process, but when they started to hear back from customers about the high level of support they were now receiving, they could see the benefit of the process. They were also better enabled to do their jobs.'

The conclusion

What the above examples show is that there are a number of reasons why people see the need to change their business model during the life of their company.

It is important to plan, but it is also important to recognize the need to adapt a business model over time as conditions change or you see better ways to add value. It may be necessary to change something about the way the product is delivered. It may be about spotting the problem in the plan for expansion.

It might, as Moo.com and Twitter discovered, be the basic premise of the business that needs to be rethought, or even a change needed in order to survive.

Other changes may need to be made to the way cash is generated by the business. If you can get cash quickly into the business then you can avoid the need for further working capital to grow operations.

One of the key points of this chapter is to be open to the need for change and to grab the opportunities when they arise.

If, like Alicia at Skimlinks, you see a chance to pivot, just do it. It will probably not be easy, but it is better to have tried and failed than to have never tried at all.

Chapter Six
You cannot cut your way to success

One of the pleasures of covering entrepreneurship for the *Financial Times* since 2005 has been the energy and positive spirit I have found among people whose passion is to build the most successful businesses they can.

Never was this more obvious than on 15 September 2008, when Lehman Brothers announced it was filing for bankruptcy protection. The reaction in the FT newsroom to what still is the world's largest bankruptcy filing was, like across the rest of the world, one of shocked disbelief. People had to get on with reporting the news, but the mood among the reporting teams was markedly more sombre than usual. Down the River Thames at Canary Wharf, the scenes being broadcast around the world were even more depressing. The footage on the television screens was of former Lehman staff packing the things on their desks into cardboard boxes and filing out of the company's European headquarters. This was a black news day indeed.

It just so happened, however, that on that particular Monday morning I had to get across town to University College London in Bloomsbury, where the staff of Seedcamp, an incubator for early-stage companies from across Europe and the Middle East, were gathering for the first day of a week-long event. The mood here, among the founders, angel investors and seasoned entrepreneurs taking part, could not have been more different from the one I had left behind at my office.

At Seedcamp, whose model is similar to the highly successful Y Combinator incubator programme in the United States, everything is believed to be possible. All the 100 or so people squeezed into one of UCL's science lecture halls that black Monday morning had come to hear a score or more fledgling businesses try to explain how they planned to make the future a much brighter place. Everyone was clapped – those leading the programme, those presenting and those just along for the ride – and afterwards the organizers waxed lyrical about the quality of the contestants. At the start of what was to be the worst recession the world had known in at least 60 years, here was a bubble of optimism. The teams of founders taking part believed that they had the best opportunity ever to create industry-changing business models that would go to make them and their backers rich beyond their wildest dreams.

It is this kind of optimism that drives entrepreneurship forward. It is the attitude you need to create a business and sustain it through the seemingly endless list of problems you will face as you struggle through those first five years that about 80 per cent of new ventures fail to survive.

Yet it is difficult to maintain this optimism when the whole economy turns south.

How do you react to the bad times?

During times of recession the pressure to cut jobs can be immense. If your bank calls in the overdraft facility that was providing working capital and there seem to be no other ways to borrow, cash needs to be managed carefully.

In hard times, cost cutting becomes a central concern for the typical business owner. First to go are the little perks like the free coffee and cake. Then it is the annual pay rise. But it soon turns to more drastic medicine.

Plenty of businesses have had to do this in recent years. They may well have to consider doing it again. The best advice for those who truly have no choice is, if you do feel compelled to cut, cut quickly and cut deep enough that you will not have to do it again for a long time.

Do you really need to make those cuts?

The question for rebel entrepreneurs, however, is whether this kind of rationing is in fact rational behaviour when you are trying to grow an enterprise. Those optimistic entrepreneurs, who were in such abundance that day in September 2008 at Seedcamp, may have something to teach the rest of us about attitude.

This chapter looks at an alternative view to the cost-cutting model, one pursued by many successful fast-growing businesses that suggests there is another way.

Shortly after Lehman Brothers filed for bankruptcy, I was contacted by a company called Netcel, which specializes in website and intranet development for trade associations. The business, based just north of London in St Albans, had not suffered from falling orders despite the difficult economic conditions at the time. Trade associations came to Netcel for services, and these organizations could not cut back on maintaining their websites. They were more stable than consumer or corporate customers because they were funded through membership payments, which did not tend to drop off suddenly, even in a banking crisis. However, Netcel was facing a cash squeeze due to problems with its clients stretching payment times to save themselves money.

Nigel Culkin, one of the company's two non-executive directors, explained the situation to me. He admitted that one of the options on the table at the time was to cut the headcount from 22 staff to 14. 'What we were looking at was real cash flow problems,' he explained. 'We said that we would need to look at making some redundancies if nothing came in.' However, the board decided against retrenchment, rightly reasoning that redundancy notices would only lower morale and further weaken the business.

Instead the executives made a dash for growth. At the time, when governments were busy bailing out the world's largest banks to prevent a collapse of the global economy, such positive thinking might have seemed wildly optimistic. But Netcel's management pulled it off. Tim Parfitt, Netcel's managing director, worked with the heads of each of the company's product group areas and identified 45 initiatives, described as 'small shiny things', which could make a material difference to cash flow.

Some were small moves, such as making more efficient use of management reports at board meetings. Others were more fundamental, such as introducing a 20 per cent up front payment once a contract was signed. The latter bore fruit in the space of two months when the signing of two contracts totalling £230,000 brought an instant cash injection of £46,000. 'If these projects had not come in, I believe we wouldn't have had any choice but to make redundancies,' Nigel explained me.

'In no way is this rocket science, but as someone once said to me, the trouble with common sense is that it's not that common. Certainly not in these troubled times.'

Sell on the savings your company can provide

One way to succeed in difficult times is to have a business model that can help others save money or give them a better return for their outlay. A classic example of this is Criteo, a clever technology company started in France in 2005 by a serial entrepreneur called JB Rudelle, a computer science graduate called Romain Niccoli and a software engineer from Microsoft called Franck Le Ouay. The company's phenomenal success is testament to how the internet can disrupt an existing industry. In Criteo's case the target market was the advertising sector, where it could improve the returns to clients by making better use of information.

Say you visit an online shop, browse through some items but decide not to buy anything. If that shop is a Criteo customer, it will then post those products on banner adverts in other websites you visit, reminding you, the consumer, about what you had previously shopped for and maybe persuading you to buy it this time. In fact, many people do go back and purchase and Criteo, being a technology company, has compiled the data to prove it.

Criteo is not the only company to do this, but it has out-executed its competition. Moreover, with special relevance to this chapter, it made a particularly aggressive drive for growth as the world economy went into the recession. In 2008, as the downturn began, Criteo's sales were €1 m. Twelve months later that had risen to €15 m, and by the end of 2011 this was up to €150 m with operations in more than 20 countries.

I met with Pascal Gauthier, the company's chief operating officer, to discuss how such growth could happen in such difficult times. He admitted that, although the founders may not have realized it at the time they started, Criteo's service was perfect for the recession because it could show real returns on advertising at a time when most people felt customers would not buy. In traditional advertising, he explained, spending decisions are often based on relationships between clients and particular salespeople because it is so difficult to see what return a certain campaign produces. Criteo could differentiate itself by providing an exact figure on how many extra sales its service was producing because the click-throughs from shoppers were all recorded.

More importantly for Criteo, it could prove that the returns were good. It could show that banner ads serviced by its technology had six times the click-through rates of conventional banner ads. In difficult times, when advertising budgets were being squeezed, figures like this were music to the ears of Criteo customers. 'It is a magic business model, like Google,' Pascal said, adding that 98 per cent of Criteo's customers have stuck with the service.

It is perhaps not surprising, therefore, that Criteo quickly became profitable and has since been able to use that money to expand operations further, opening a headquarters in Palo Alto and bringing in some big hitters from the Silicon Valley technology crowd. It is in many ways a virtuous circle of repeat sales from existing customers and new business in new markets from online retailers desperate to get a bang for their advertising buck. In this kind of scenario, who wouldn't invest more to grow, even when times are hard?

The lesson from Criteo is that if you have an opportunity to sell as a money-saving or revenue-raising service during hard times, then you should use it.

For others, the opportunity might not be as obvious as it was for Criteo, and their approach may involve tweaking the business model a little. However, that does not mean it is not worth trying.

Another person who refused to succumb to the temptation to cut back during tough times was Jim Sproat. His Glasgow-based technology business, Community People – which trades under the name Organised Feedback – had discovered a lucrative niche enabling local councils to hold online consultations with their local taxpayers. By 2010, councils in the UK were themselves making significant cuts as part of the British government's push to reduce the country's enormous budget deficit. In fact Jim told me that his company's revenue had dropped by 40 per cent between 2009 and 2011.

But rather than attempting to cut his coat to suit his cloth, as the English saying goes, Jim and his three other directors went out and metaphorically bought themselves a new set of clothes by seeking new business opportunities. In fact, they spent £50,000 to turn their core product into an electronic suggestion box. This the company marketed as a way to get council employees to highlight money-saving measures in the town hall. At a stroke the owners of Community People turned their business from one that provided something local authorities saw as a good but non-essential item into a business that was a compelling offering to cash-strapped councils, even providing a way to save taxpayers money.

When I spoke to Jim it was still only a few weeks after he had unveiled his new venture, but Community People had already signed

up two councils for the service and had 15 other authorities express-
ing an interest. 'We were losing public sector business and we knew
we would lose more, so we needed ideas,' Jim boasted. 'If we had
continued doing what we were doing, there is a chance we might not
still be around.'

Cost cutting may become the order of the day again for many
small businesses, but Jim told me this was difficult at Community
People because it was already a fairly lean organization. (This is
probably true for a lot of other young businesses that have not yet
had time to accumulate a lot of extra costs.) Community People
comprises just four directors and three software developers.
Marketing costs are kept to a minimum by using social media and
personal recommendations to spread the word about the products.
Its address in Prestwick, on the edge of Glasgow, is only an office for
Jim, since the rest of the team do their work remotely – the development team is spread between Dublin, Manchester and India.

Although the market was still tough for Community People, and
local authorities in the UK continue to have to tighten their belts, Jim
told me he was confident that his business had a bigger future with
its new product.

Another thing he did was to look for new markets. In Jim's case,
having specialized in public sector work, there was a potentially
much bigger opportunity in the private sector. When I spoke to
him he had received some interest from Standard Life in India. He
was also looking for resellers to market the software in the United
States.

Expanding your way out of a downturn is not easy, however. Jim
was able to use some existing cash in the business to fund the new
systems development, but he and his fellow directors also had to dig
into their own pockets to make up the shortfall. 'We did have to bite
the bullet,' he told me.

Another believer in seeing opportunities in troubled times is David
Lewis, owner and director of Camrose Consulting. He is a great
believer in the idea that you cannot cut your way to success. 'Those

businesses that move into a slash-and-burn mentality when things get tough are likely to be short sighted,' he explained.

My experience while covering the small business sector during the 2008 recession offers support for this view. I came across many companies that felt forced to cut costs when the recession started, only to find that they had burdened themselves with further problems, most notably demoralized staff and the risk that competitors could gain an advantage over them while they were weakened.

Hugh Robertson, chief executive of London-based marketing agency RPM, was one of the lucky ones during the downturn. In 2010 the company generated revenue of over £25m, and in 2011, when I spoke to the founders, it had not yet suffered a drop in sales despite years of economic malaise – although Hugh admitted to me that clients were looking to see increased returns on the money they were spending on campaigns.

Like those mentioned before in this chapter, Hugh claimed that cutting costs was not the correct response to difficult times. Instead, he focused his efforts on getting good forecasts of trends in the market in which his business operated, then communicating that information clearly and openly to his staff, and finally involving them in the process of making the business operate more efficiently. This was not a simple matter given that RPM employed about 180 people at its headquarters in a converted treacle factory in Shepherds Bush, west London.

Hugh claimed that, despite its growth, RPM maintained the meritocratic values of a start-up. These were very important to him, since he had founded the business with two other media industry executives as a reaction against the way large media agencies in London operated. Their aim was to provide a viable alternative through a smaller company, or at least one with what he saw as the virtues of small company operations.

An example of this, he suggested, is the monthly company-wide meeting, where everyone can be updated on the financial performance of the business. These get-togethers are actually used for a lot more than information dissemination. They are an opportunity to introduce new starters, highlight recent successes and failures in the business, and outline changes in working policy. Hugh explained that his aim was 'to make people part of the journey, not just employees', and thus more motivated. In doing so, he showed that running a business could, and perhaps should, be about a lot more than just making money.

Of course, by enthusing the staff about the business and making them feel involved in the key decision-making moments, Hugh encouraged his employees to take ownership of what they were doing and thus earn the business a lot more money. It was just that he did not put the economic cart before the horse.

Robin Burman, RPM's finance director, was more explicit about the commercial importance of engaging staff. 'Businesses work most effectively as a team, so we would talk to staff directly about difficult economic conditions, declining sales and reductions in profit and work as resourcefully as we can together,' he told me. 'In a service business, where people are your capital, redundancies must be a last resort, as inevitably you will also incur [the cost of] hiring sprees.'

RPM was also a long way from its origins, as Hugh and his co-founders had set up the agency in a former cow shed in Wokingham, in the home counties, south west of London. Hugh told me that the company had succeeded in large part because it had operated differently from its peers. One got the feeling that even if there were cuts to be made at RPM, they would be a lot easier to deal with because everyone felt decision making was democratic. However, this had yet to be tested when I spoke to Hugh and Robin.

Gerard Burke of YBYF, whom we have met in previous chapters, only teaches ambitious entrepreneurs. Over the years, however, he has worked with hundreds of these companies and so can be said to have some valuable experience. And when it comes to the issue of cuts, he is convinced that cutting back in hard times is false wisdom. 'In tough economic times, some owner-managers will simply hunker down and stop all investments,' he explained. 'Whilst this preserves cash in the short term, it restricts the ability to grasp the upside of the downturn and is de-motivating for everyone in the business.'

Winners continue to take what Gerard calls 'wise' investments for the future. This will mean different things for different owners and different companies, but Gerard believes everyone can find what is right for them by taking some simple steps. 'You need a clear plan for the future you want to create for your business and yourself,' he told me. 'You then need the realism to differentiate between those investments that are crucial to bringing that future about and those that do not really need to be made.'

Gerard, like many people who advise a lot of businesses, is a great believer in the concept of 'sticking to the knitting', or doing what you do best as a company. Rebel entrepreneurs are not only good at this, they are good at self-analysis to see if they can do the things they are good at better. When times are tough, it is important to look at whether you have exploited all of your existing niches as a business, because (as has been said in previous chapters) it is easier to sell more of your existing products and services to your existing customers and people who are like them. It is also likely that such strategies will be more profitable and far less risky than looking to create new markets for your enterprise.

Gerard told me that, in his experience, successful companies are those that continue to invest in their people no matter what the conditions in the market they operate. 'Even if they've had to lay some people off, they will invest in the people who remain to ensure they are motivated and appropriately skilled,' he told me.

One way you can cleverly develop your staff for little or no cost, while increasing morale, is to get them to take responsibility for helping one another. If budgets are cut for training and development, why not get people to shadow colleagues or teach one another in lunchtime sessions?

The FT has been doing this since before I joined the company in 1999, getting experienced journalists to share their insights over a plate of sandwiches and a PowerPoint presentation. Over the years, these 'masterclasses', as they are called, have covered everything from the obvious, such as news writing, to the more specialist, such as using databases to dig for stories and how to get the most out of a Twitter account as a commentator on a specific industry or geographic region.

In a smaller organization, you might get back office staff to go out with sales staff so they learn the ropes.

This strategy can achieve two objectives: motivating people on the front line of your business to be teachers of others and creating career paths for people who might have thought they had none.

Spend some money on yourself

Gerard said he also believes that successful business owners need to invest in themselves as well as their staff. Again, this is especially important when times get tough, he told me. 'They know that they need to maintain their own passion, energy and drive. And sometimes, that means stepping out of the business for short periods to re-charge and re-focus.'

Perhaps unsurprisingly, Gerard recommends his own course for owner-managers to achieve this. However, this is not the only option. Many rebel entrepreneurs learn how to become better in their role through one-to-one coaching, either through a formal club or through people with whom they have 'clicked'. It is even possible by network-ing with other entrepreneurs, and a range of business groups in many countries have been created with the sole intention of doing just this. It is often not so much a case of finding one of these, but finding one that suits your state of business growth, ambition or particular industry specialism.

Some of these groups – such as BNI, which claims to be the world's largest networking group for business owners – are not really about personal development so much as generating sales. BNI has become an enormous global network because it is very good at what it does, which is getting business owners to feed leads and recommend one another. However, it also has restrictions, such as the fact that two people with the same business cannot be members of the same BNI chapter.

The kinds of truly ambitious rebel entrepreneurs I am talking about in this book are also likely to outgrow a group like BNI. More appropriate may be the private members' groups, such as The Supper Club in the UK, which are specifically aimed at ambitious entrepreneurs and have rules, such as 'what's said in the room, stays in the room', to ensure that founders can speak openly about their most pressing concerns. The key strength of groups like this is the value of peer learning from those who have probably been through exactly the same problems that you have.

Another very successful group is The Entrepreneurial Exchange, which has become the pre-eminent networking organization for founders in Scotland. Its aim is to inspire, motivate, educate and support ambitious entrepreneurs to achieve their full potential. The organization began in 1994 with 50 founder members, and now has over 400 members, whose companies collectively employ more than 290,000 people and generate sales of over £23 bn. Its membership list reads like a *Who's Who* of Scottish business, a testament in itself to the importance of such networking to the best entrepreneurs.

Like The Supper Club, The Entrepreneurial Exchange thrives by creating an environment where founders can learn from other founders. In the lonely world of building a company, these are highly prized opportunities to learn more and should be grabbed by any aspiring entrepreneur.

Be confident

Growth is often about confidence, and confidence is one of the most important characteristics of a successful entrepreneur, according to Gerard Burke. When times are tough, it is easy to get caught in the short-term requirements of survival, but this can be dispiriting for both you and your staff, he told me. 'It is important to look beyond the short term and have a confident and clear view of the medium to longer term,' Gerard said. 'Stay confident about what makes your business great. Stay confident about your passion for your business. Stay confident about the future you will create for your business and yourself.'

It is also important to communicate this confidence to your employees. This is what charismatic rebel entrepreneurs often do best. 'This confidence will spread to your staff, to your customers and to your suppliers,' Gerard explained. 'The effect will be dramatic.'

Do not rush to cut jobs

If you do have to make cuts to corporate budgets, you can still expand your company's headcount, making it stronger for the eventual upturn. You just need to be clever about how you save money.

One way to save money while preserving jobs is, of course, to just cut everyone's salary. It is an excellent way to meet two apparently conflicting objectives – saving money and maintaining staffing levels – but it needs to be handled carefully.

Dyson, the bagless cylinder vacuum cleaner business, was another company that decided it needed to economize as the world went into recession in 2008. It did this, cutting the overall salary bill from £98.9m to £92.8m. Founder Sir James Dyson led from the front, cutting his annual salary from £12.5m to £457,000.

This might seem small beer for such a high earner, and Sir James, while not chief executive, remains the highest-paid member of staff at Dyson. However, as a result of his actions, Sir James was able to provide some good news for the company at a time when everyone was aware that people in other companies would be facing redundancy. In fact, Dyson was able to increase its overall staff headcount from 2,203 to 2,461. Presumably this made the announcement that salaries were falling across the business a little more palatable for those involved.

This is not to say that Dyson has not made job cuts in the past. In 2002, Sir James was roundly criticized by the UK media when he made the difficult decision to move the manufacture of his products to Malaysia. The anger was righteous. The move cost almost 800 jobs from the company's headquarters in Malmesbury, ironically where Jamie Murray Wells started his Glasses Direct business. Sir James has since pointed out that he had wanted to expand his operations in the UK, but was prevented from doing so by the local council. If production had not been moved abroad, the company would have had to shut, he claimed.

Such cuts, however, are something of an exception at Dyson. Since moving production to Malaysia, Dyson has been able to create many more jobs in design at its Malmesbury base. Sometimes it seems a cut can actually help a business grow in other ways. The lesson from Dyson here is that you cut costs in the areas that generate least value while investing in those that create the future wealth of the business.

Dyson spends a lot of money to keep its designs ahead of the competition. In 2010, while the British economy was still struggling to get out of recession, Dyson spent almost £1 m a week on research and development.

Find the opportunities to grow

A key point for rebel entrepreneurs is to remember that even in difficult times there are probably ways for your business to grow if you can find them. These may well need investment, but it is money that could pay back a return quickly.

Another business owner who had to deal with the choice of cutting or expanding in the face of a shrinking market was David Macken, managing director of System Associates, mentioned in Chapter 3. After the 2010 UK general election, when the new coalition government of Conservatives and Liberal Democrats introduced one of the developed world's tightest spending squeezes, David's central government customers stopped spending almost overnight. The way that many contracts were dropped was also far from well managed, and involved wasted conversations with civil servants who knew they lacked the funds to pay System Associates before they started talking, David told me. 'On one occasion, we went for a kick-off meeting for a project, only to be told three-quarters of the way through that they had no money to spend on the work.'

The cuts posed a major problem as half of the company's revenues came from contracts with Whitehall departments. It was not an easy time for David. He decided to make 6 of his 20 employees redundant to bring down his cost base.

However, David is not a man to be beaten. Instead of trying to persuade government departments to change their ways, he got his team to focus on finding new clients that did have the money to spend. They did not have to look far for opportunities. In their case, there were changes to sell to organizations on the fringe of the public sector, such as Wales Co-operative, a centre that manages a number of Welsh social enterprises. These contracts were typically in the £100,000 range, compared with the £300,000 deals System Associates was used to winning with central government. But the extra business enabled System Associates to reduce its reliance on the public sector, cutting the percentage of revenue it gained from these clients from 90 per cent to 75 per cent.

Although the loss of central government work was hard for the business to cope with, the realignment of operations and the focus on new opportunities meant that revenue at the end of 2010 was only down 10 per cent, though profit fell 20 per cent. Moreover, the new business created a growing market for System Associates. David told me that sales from his new markets would help lift revenues by 40 per cent in the 2011/12 financial year. 'We haven't given up on government,' he said, adding that he hoped his company would pick up contracts as a supplier that can do more with less money.

David did not just look for the quick gains from low-hanging fruit in new markets. He also spent money on his company's long-term future. He took the bold decision to invest in the next generation of web technologies through a research project with nearby Reading

University, one of the world's leading research institutes in this area. He borrowed £150,000 to help fund the research but justified this to me by his expectation that the results would give his business a set of products that would make it less reliant on the public sector.

Remember to pivot as well as invest

Another company that had to adapt itself to the UK's government spending cuts is Etc Venues, which provides corporate training facilities for organizations. It also managed to grow its business by changing its pitch subtly. In doing so, it performed a kind of pivot, like the ones discussed in the previous chapter.

About a quarter of Etc's business is with public sector bodies, so it too saw a dramatic decline in revenue during the UK government's spending squeeze. However, it has managed to recoup a lot of the losses by pitching itself as a low-cost alternative for taxpayer-funded bodies that previously paid more for expensive training locations, such as hotels and conference centres. Etc also refocused its efforts on marketing its strengths as a provider of high-quality training facilities to set itself apart from those that provide little more than a room with tea and coffee. As a result, the business was able to bring in new, in some ways better-quality, public sector customers, although it must be said that in this case it did not entirely offset the decline in business from others cancelling contracts.

However, Etc went beyond its core audience of government bodies and found opportunities in the private sector. It had particular success among professional services firms and banks, which, after several years of belt-tightening in the wake of the financial crisis, had begun to spend money again on off-site staff training.

Confidence was clearly not in short supply when I spoke to Alastair Stewart, Etc's managing director, in 2011. 'There is still a huge amount of money being spent,' he said, adding that it was a matter of knowing where to find it. 'Although we have seen the revenue drop from the public sector, there are ways and means of dealing with it.'

The retrenching of the UK government in the face of unsustainable public sector deficits is having an effect on various British businesses and raising the pressure to cut costs to survive. And it is not just the UK that is having to make public sector cuts. The squeeze on public spending across the developed world has forced many companies to reduce their reliance on the public sector for business.

Fortunately, many have found it entirely possible to pick up contracts elsewhere. One example is Wilson Sherriff, a training and coaching provider. Again it was hit by the UK government's spending clampdown. Before the cuts were announced, the company relied on the public sector for 90 per cent of its revenues. However, in the space of a year it was able to bring this down to just half of its income and, amazingly, it was able to do this without a drop in overall sales.

The trick, according to co-founder Carol Sherriff, was to increase the sales effort for private sector business that was already showing some traction before the public sector cuts began to bite.

One of the most fruitful areas of new business for Wilson Sherriff was with multinational companies that need to bring employees from around the world together in one place. Wilson Sherriff had experience in doing just this, so was able to find leads for more contracts. 'We started with people who we knew, then we went with people who knew us and were recommending us to other people,' Carol told me.

In many ways, what is happening to these companies is what happens to every business at some point: the market changes and you need to refocus your selling efforts on new opportunities. The main lesson seems to be that the best opportunities are often not too far away from where you have already been operating. However, it is important to seize the chances quickly before your business is forced to cut back and so lose the skill base that gives it a competitive edge.

One thing to remember is that it is just as bad to avoid necessary cuts as it is to make unnecessary ones.

Of course, there are times when cuts are unavoidable. However, even when this is the only alternative it is possible to use cuts to make a business more productive and therefore give it the ability to expand to the next level. As every good gardener knows, you regularly have to trim back plants in order to give them the means to grow bigger. In fact, if you do not prune, you may never see growth. Therefore cuts can be a way of making something stronger. Business is no exception to this rule.

James Hibbert, founder of Dress2Kill, a modern bespoke tailoring service based in central London, literally knows about cutting one's coat according to one's cloth. I have known James and his business for several years, not least because his main office is a short stroll from the *Financial Times*.

I first met James at Adams Street, a private members' club in the West End, which over the last decade has gained a reputation as a hang-out for London's ambitious entrepreneurs to unwind and meet like-minded individuals. James had quit a high flying career in the City to pursue his dream of entrepreneurship and believed that, with his model for creating bespoke tailoring at a fraction of the prices charged on Savile Row, he could bring around a new interest in tailored workwear among British men.

The banking industry collapse in 2008 hit his business hard and, in the space of nine months, James was forced to close 2 of his 3 shops and make 8 of his 20 staff redundant. This was not easy for a man with big ambitions. At the time, he had only recently expanded his enterprise's physical space and here was Dress2Kill reduced to the one outlet James had started with several years before.

However, this founder, who always seems to have a smile on his face, was not going to take matters lying down. It is hard to find a successful entrepreneur who remains gloomy for long. James called me up, almost boasting about how the recession had forced him to toughen up. While he had been forced to downsize his operations, he had also been looking to see if he could make production better as well as cheaper.

He achieved this by finding low-cost production sources in India, introduced to him through one of his London employees who hailed from the subcontinent. The cloth was still made in Britain, the measuring up could still be done in the shop, but the garments were made thousands of miles away at a fraction of the cost of British stitchers. Thanks to the many logistics routes between the UK and India, James could get a garment between the two countries in a matter of days, hardly altering the time it took to make the suits.

No one could accuse James of being unpatriotic. He would boast that Dress2Kill sourced its cloth from only one manufacturer, in the Yorkshire city of Huddersfield. (This was also a canny commercial arrangement as it enabled Dress2Kill to get better prices through bulk purchases.)

James insisted to me that shrinking his business had made the enterprise better able to grab opportunities created by what were tough times to sell an upmarket piece of clothing. When Lehman Brothers collapsed in September 2008, sales had evaporated and the business had made a loss of £50,000 in one month. A year later, however, with its new, lower cost base and more efficient way of working, Dress2Kill made a net profit of £250,000. 'We cut back once and then we cut again, but we made the business leaner and leaner,' James explained to me.

The new, lean operation was a reversal of James's strategy of just a year previously. Then he had been opening a shop on Jermyn Street, London's Mecca for high-quality menswear and second only to Savile Row as a centre for tailoring. At the time, sales were booming. The problem was that the expansion had shackled Dress2Kill with high overheads and a lack of liquidity. 'Our cash was tied up in suits,' James told me, adding that one of his first jobs when the crunch came was to fire the bookkeeper who failed to warn him that his actions had raised such risks. Dress2Kill's cuts meant that its overheads fell from £70,000 to £30,000 in six months. However, the result was that, a few months later, the business reported its best sales month in 10 years.

Even when forced to make cuts, a business like Dress2Kill can also find the opportunity to invest money to grow during those straitened times. James paid a company to transform Dress2Kill's website into a virtual tailor's shop, allowing customers to input their own measurements and have a bespoke suit delivered to their door in just 14 days. Again this raised the productivity of the business, generating sales without the cost of additional Dress2Kill staff or premises. In effect the customers became part of the staff by measuring themselves, with a little guidance from instructions on the website.

None of this takes away from the fact that the process of reorganizing Dress2Kill was very painful. Having gone through his own personal baptism of fire, however, James believed he had learnt some important lessons. The most important one was he did not need three shops to serve a single city with handmade suits, even one the size of London. 'We were robbing Peter to pay Paul,' he said to me.

For many small companies, survival is about cutting costs. The danger, however, is that you cut the wrong costs, saving you money but threatening your company's very existence. I have come across plenty of examples of this.

The easiest cuts are not always the right ones. When Fast Track Holidays, a call-centre-based travel agency, saw business slow down, founder Robin Deller's first reaction was to cut the marketing budget by 30 per cent. This was understandable, as marketing was half of the company's overhead. But that did not make it the right decision.

'Sometimes you get scared,' he told me. 'The thing with marketing was that it was one of those things that you could cut immediately – you don't need to plan an exit.'

Fast Track had grown fast, building a turnover of £40m and a staff of 130 people in four years. However, as revenues grew, costs seemed to rise even faster, and Robin told me that he noticed customers were moving from buying holidays over Teletext (the UK's old analogue television information service, where Fast Track was dominant) to the internet. At the time, Robin said, he was frightened at the large amount of money being spent solely on marketing. 'I found I started looking at figures that I was uncomfortable with because, in my own life, I would not be dealing with large sums like that,' he explained. He later realized this naivety may have been due to the fact that his particular skill was selling, rather than finance.

Fortunately for Robin, he found a good financial adviser in the form of Colin Mills, founder of the FD Centre, a supplier of part-time finance directors. Colin told Robin to reinstate his marketing spending and target it at the media that produced the highest return on investment. In Fast Track's case, that meant spending a lot of the money on national newspaper advertising, even though it was one of the most expensive channels to use.

During the next two years, Fast Track's profits rose by over 1,000 per cent, which allowed Robin to sell the business to Virgin Holidays for a seven-figure sum.

Adam Starkey, founder of Green Gourmet – a supplier of high-quality frozen foods to schools, local authorities and leisure centres – told me that his problem was not so much cutting costs as refusing to spend on costs that would be good for his Cotswolds business. 'At one point, I was obsessed with the production costs and maximizing the percentage gross margin I made per item,' he said. 'I was designing the production lines myself and being a jack of all trades.' However, this self-sufficiency created a bottleneck for the business because Adam had no spare capacity to develop new products or find new customers.

Fortunately, Adam is someone who is prepared to change his mind. He started Green Gourmet in the 1990s, driven by his vegetarian beliefs. But since then he admitted to himself that he also liked the taste of meat – if it is well prepared. So he eventually stopped trying to do everything in-house and sub-contracted production to 12 factories, liberating him to develop new products and markets. 'They were better than me at running factories and I was better than them at understanding what markets wanted,' he told me. 'As a result, the business has the most flexible cost base of any manufacturer, with the ability to triple in size in three years.'

Adam admitted to me that he only made the change long after he was advised to do so by wiser experts. 'It was my controlling nature that ruled my decision making rather than common sense,' he said.

Even apparently common-sense cost cuts can backfire. Harry Lyon-Smith has been a director of Illustration – an agency of about 200 illustrators and animators working in the UK, the United States,

Hamburg, Paris and Singapore – for over 13 years. He admitted to making a 'silly, expensive mistake' at the beginning of the current credit crunch. Harry and his colleagues decided to move their web server from the UK to Germany because they calculated that it could save the business a few hundred pounds a month.

In reality, the move resulted in a halving of the company's traffic from the United States because Illustration was no longer getting top billing on American Google searches. 'The German company was very efficient, but what I didn't realize was that Google results are based on the proximity of the servers to the people making the search,' he told me. This meant that Illustration fell below the first page of search results on Google when people in the United States searched for illustrators, having previously been at the top of the listings. 'Business dropped, which we thought was just the economy. But I am now sure we lost tens of thousands of dollars because, now that we have restored the Google ranking using expensive proxy servers, business is improving.'

One of the most expensive mistakes can be to try to save money on key people, according to James Layfield, a serial entrepreneur. One of his early businesses was a marketing agency called The Lounge. In an effort to save money when launching the venture, James and his business partner decided to save the £75,000 cost of hiring a client services director. Later he confessed to me that the company paid far more than this as a result, because its client retention rate dropped to almost zero. 'Everyone knows that keeping existing customers is a lot cheaper than getting new business,' he recalled. 'We found we had to crank up our own work 100-fold, just to win new business.'

Many owner-managers have used the global recession to reinvent themselves and, perhaps, even make their ventures stronger as a result. Paul Welch, co-founder of London-based brokerage Large Mortgage Loans, is one of those. His solution to the collapse in the housing market in the UK was to become more focused on his niche, striking a partnership with mass-market estate agents such as Countrywide, and private banks such as Coutts, offering to share any fees if they passed on clients in need of substantial mortgages.

Paul told me he had no choice. Turnover, which had been doubling in each of the first five years of trading, dropped from £1.2m to £500,000 during 2009. The phones stopped ringing, he admitted.

Not that Paul's wife was best pleased when he said the financial squeeze meant that they and their two-year-old daughter would have to move home. They gave up a smart apartment in London's upmarket Canary Wharf development for a dramatically cheaper place in the middle of an Essex council estate next door to Lakeside, a mega mall with little soul or character.

Neither were his 23 employees. Those who did not resign or get made redundant had to take a pay cut, from as much as £50,000 a year to the minimum wage level of £12,000, topped up with commission.

It was a matter of survival, Paul told me, pointing out that monthly overheads dropped by a third to £20,000 at a stroke. While cutting costs was essential for survival in the short term, Paul said the measures he took to build the business also meant it had a brighter future and was able to grow much more than it did before he made the changes. Turnover was on track to reach about £1m when I spoke to him in 2010.

Large Mortgage Loans was able to count premiership footballers, Hollywood actors and pop singers among its clientele as their fortunes largely remained unscathed by the global recession. 'We have always been innovative,' Paul told me, noting that his business had pioneered the idea of texting a quote to clients three years earlier. 'But what has happened is that [the recession] has forced me to be more innovative, perhaps obsessively so.'

Another case of entrepreneurs having change forced on them is that of Martin Stocks, David Deiraniya and John James. Until April 2010, the three men had been running a successful office furniture dealership called the Momentum Group, which they had built from scratch in 1991 to a turnover of about £23m and 70 staff. But then GE Commercial Finance, which had supplied the company with invoice discounting finance since 2001, turned off the funding tap and installed accountants BDO Stoy Hayward to conduct a review of the company's future. Within four weeks the business, which had offices in the London neighbourhoods of Putney, Clerkenwell and Shoreditch, was being put into administration.

Martin told me that the experience had left him and his co-founders 'pretty scarred' and bitter – particularly since it had come after Momentum had already gone through three rounds of redundancies to keep its costs down. However, he and his business partners refused to be beaten. Instead, they formed a new company, Operandum, which focused on the one area of the old business that the three founders felt had most traction, helping companies procure furniture. 'Between the three of us, we have a very strong working relationship,' Martin told me, noting that his skills in finance and general management complement the sales talents of his fellow founders. 'Before, we had a complex set of five companies. But with that taken away from us, we felt that we had an opportunity to do something that wasn't being done elsewhere.'

What is good for the goose, however, is not always good for the gander. Operandum enabled Martin and his business partners to escape. But the same was not true for its suppliers. Martin and his team managed to convince most of them to continue trading with them. Martin told me that it was important to maintain your honesty and integrity in such situations. However, in business such ethics are difficult to maintain. The insolvency process often creates winners and losers. In the case of Operandum, there were suppliers that felt burnt by the experience.

One of those was in fact a subsidiary of Momentum, a nearby office removals and relocation business called Function. Its manager, Tony Factor, came to speak to me at the time and explained the situation. As Momentum was Function's principal shareholder, when it brought in the administrators Tony faced the real prospect of insolvency himself.

BDO Stoy Hayward invited Tony to look at the option of liquidation or a pre-packaged administration for Function. However, calling it a day was not an option he told me. 'Here is a business that I have been running for five or six years – it was well respected, we had all worked really hard and we had been profitable throughout,' he said at the time.

But while entering insolvency would have been relatively easy, avoiding it was far more difficult. Firstly, all £350,000 of Function's cash reserves had gone. A third of that money belonged to Tony personally. GE, which had started the trouble for Momentum, was also Function's invoice factoring supplier, its main source of financing. When it stopped funding Momentum, it stopped funding Function and all the other subsidiaries.

Tony's first concern, though, was his dozen staff, who he needed to be on-side with his rescue plan. 'We have values that we hold close in this company,' he told me. 'The key value is communicating honestly and openly, so everybody knows where we are.'

When I went to visit Function's offices, Tony showed me the long sheet of paper stuck to the wall of the company's boardroom, containing comments from a staff meeting to discuss the crisis seven months previously. It was filled with dozens of neon-yellow and electric-pink stars with little celebrations of life in the business, such as 'finding the sausage stall' – a reference to a nearby street market that became a regular lunchtime haunt. 'When we looked at what we had done, and what our clients thought of us, we realized we couldn't lose this,' Tony told me.

He also had similar conversations with Function's 20 key suppliers. 'I said we owe you X, we are determined to pay you, but you need to help us and we are going to stretch you to breaking point.'

Although Tony was clearly hurt by what had happened to Function because of Operandum's actions he spoke the same language as his company's former owners. At Operandum, Martin had told me: 'However tough the scenario you are going through, you have got to maintain your honesty and integrity because what goes around comes around.' Tony similarly stressed the importance of openness and honesty in Function's moment of crisis. 'We lost a physical business,' Martin said. 'But what we had of significant value was our 18-year working relationship with the clients who remained loyal to us, the relationships with suppliers that would still work with us and the knowledge of what would work in the market.' Tony told me that he provided a personal guarantee, to any supplier that requested it, that he would repay them if the company faced further trouble.

Getting the support of these businesses, many of which were 'one driver and a van' operations, was crucial because Function relied on their support to cope with spikes in activity, especially at weekends, when more than 100 people might be required to move furniture. 'These are guys who supply vans and labour for us when we get too busy to manage it ourselves,' Tony told me. 'They are all smallish companies and if they don't get paid, they go hungry.'

Tony also needed to talk to GE because he still needed some form of invoice financing. This method of borrowing money, based on unpaid bills, was crucial to Function because of its cash flow process. Staff salaries, by far the company's largest outlay, had to be paid before customers settled their bills. By using invoice financing, Function could get cash into the business within 24 hours of the work being done.

Factor had never spoken with GE before the administration issue because the lender had provided all Function's finance through its agreement with the parent company. 'We had no relationship with GE, to the point that they thought we actually sold furniture because everybody else in the group did,' he told me. Waiting for the letter of approval for a credit line was the worst moment in the process, Tony said. It eventually came through, helped by GE already having Function's bank statements on file.

The stress, however, gave Tony an ulcer.

Operandum too survived, and indeed prospered under a new business model. In just a few weeks of trading again, the new business had picked up about £60,000 in fees, putting it on track for a turnover of £750,000 in its first year. Operandum had several advantages over Momentum, not least a much shorter buying cycle; whereas pitching to buy a company's furniture at Momentum could take as long as a year, Operandum can get hired for its service in a matter of days.

Buying and selling furniture also requires large cash reserves because customers tend to pay 30 days after delivery, whereas Operandum's work could be paid for up front. 'We now have a completely cash-neutral model,' Martin told me. With just six staff and a serviced office to run, Operandum also had much lower overheads than its forebear.

Perhaps more business owners who find themselves in such troubled circumstances would follow a similar path if they realized how much of value they retained after a corporate failure. But that is for another chapter.

The conclusion

The main point of this chapter is to say that the knee-jerk reaction to a downturn in business of cutting costs and firing staff is not necessarily the best strategy to follow.

It may be that you need to find a different way to grow the business, even changing the business model slightly.

Adjusting your business in difficult times is never going to be easy, but it may just save your livelihood and put it on a better footing for faster growth in the future.

Sometimes, as in the case of Dress2Kill, you have to cut back in some areas in order to invest in others.

You may also have to spend more money than you did before, but in the long term this could well enable your business to become a much bigger operation than it would have done.

One thing is certain. Doing nothing is not an option.

Chapter Seven
Do not waste
your time selling

Selling is at the heart of any successful business. If you cannot sell what you make, your business will go nowhere. However, it is not just your ability to sell, but your ability to sell more cleverly that will mark a great business out from the rest of the pack.

Before you start selling, however, you have to find a good salesperson, which in itself is a major headache for many founders. This might be because the founder is in fact a good salesperson and finds it hard to hand over the reins – the kind of meddler we talked about in Chapter 3. However, it is also because good salespeople are, for a number of reasons, very hard to spot and often just as hard to entice into a challenger brand that may be perceived as a more risky employment proposition.

Good people are always difficult to come by, but there are particular reasons why it is particularly tricky to get your hands on good sales-people. The first problem comes at the interview stage. A good sales-person may be able to sell him or herself very well to you and your board, but that does not mean that he or she can sell your product. The danger is that you do not realize until it is too late that you have employed a great self-publicist rather than a great salesperson. You will then face the unenviable task of getting rid of that person, a difficult process at the best of times. The bad news here is that there does not seem to be an easy way to spot those with the talent to sell for you rather than themselves.

I have already talked, in Chapter 3, about the problems Tom Woods went through in hiring a sales head for his company, dinner-cruise operator Silver Fleet. However, it is worth noting again that his solution came in the form of employing outside specialist advice for the recruitment process and not relying on personal chemistry to sway his decision when choosing a new sales director.

It may also be worth bearing in mind that often the best way to bring anyone into a business is to hire on the basis of their attitude. You can then train them for the specific role. It has often been said to me that the best salespeople, particularly those working for start-ups, are those who learn on the job, shadowing someone who is already selling to customers to see how it has been done. This is of course true for many roles, particularly in the kind of entrepreneurial businesses I am considering in this book, which are likely by their nature to do things differently to most companies.

Nurturing talent is also a matter of finding what drives people, their personal preferences and goals, giving them the opportunity to play to their strengths and enabling them to succeed. It sounds simple in theory, but in practice needs a manager's attention to an individual's needs.

Gerard Burke at YPYF has come across the issue of finding good sales heads plenty of times over the years of helping ambitious owner-managers. His advice to me was to provide regular feedback and communication with salespeople to ensure their activity stays aligned with the needs of the organization and that they feel valued. At the same time, however, he noted that transgressions must be dealt with swiftly. 'Never let yourself be held to ransom,' he said.

When it comes to finding someone to lead a sales operation, one specific piece of advice I have been given is to avoid promoting from within. It has often been said to me that good salespeople seldom make good managers.

Spotting a talent for the job, however, is just part of the problem of getting yourself a good person to run your sales function. The other big issue that many founders complain to me about is the difficulty in coaxing good salespeople away from other companies. At the heart of this problem is the reality that good salespeople tend to get well rewarded by their existing employers because they are so important to the business. You are therefore unlikely to be able to lure someone away to your business by just offering more money.

If you are a relatively young business you may also have a problem of credibility in that no one has heard of you. If you are a fast-growing business then your numbers may speak for themselves, although if you have got yourself in this position then a prospective sales head may ask what he or she can do that you have not already done.

The problem of coaxing talented sales executives over to your business is seldom made easier by the underlying economic picture. In times of recession and rising unemployment there may be more salespeople on the market but companies are unlikely to have let the good ones go. Those who are in the market for work, therefore, may not be the best talent available. If a sales executive has been made redundant, there is likely to be a reason for that and it may be because that person is just not that good at their job. If they do have talent and are looking for work, they may be more inclined to go with a large, safe business than your venture.

In the good times, the search for a good salesperson can be equally hard because it is difficult to sort the wheat from the chaff. If you are in a successful market sector, such as online retailing, where new companies generally find it relatively easy to grow, a bad salesperson may be able to mask his or her shortcomings because the product or service they are trying to sell in fact sells itself. A rising tide, after all, lifts all boats.

The final problem with finding good salespeople is to do with finding people who are good for your business at its stage of development. As I have mentioned in previous chapters, companies tend to change as they get past a certain size. The way that they sell can change too. As a result, a person who is good at selling in a large company may not be the kind of person who can sell at a smaller, albeit fast-growing, business like your own.

The uncomfortable truth about finding salespeople is that it is never likely to be easy. It helps to cast your net as widely as possible and remember that any hiring process is likely to have to be followed by a fair amount of coaching. This is going to be particularly important for any sales role.

Tips for accelerating the sales process

Hiring a great salesperson is, of course, just the start of the process of developing a great sales operation.

Another of the challenges I have come across again and again among fast-growing businesses is the issue of getting more customers, more quickly. How do you accelerate the sales process? One person who believes he has some answers is Sam Phillips, founder and chief executive of Glide Technologies, which provides web-based marketing management software for large companies that want to manage their brand online.

His business, whose customers include Sony, eBay and Barclays, increased its revenues from £2 m to £3.5 m in 2010. He was aiming to double it again when I met him that year, so any blockages in the sales cycle were a big concern. However, Glide had made some significant progress in this area. It had already managed to cut the time it took to close a deal from an average of seven months to five months, and had done this by following a few basic rules.

First, it had focused on ensuring that the sales team knew every one of the key people involved in the buying process. This usually amounted to knowing four executives: the sponsor, the financial buyer, the procurer and the user. 'The classic mistake people make is to think they have a good relationship with one person involved in buying their product and then not think of the other people,' Sam told me. It is more than just building a relationship with these key people, he added. It is nuts-and-bolts things like knowing when they go on holiday. 'All it takes is for someone to go away for a deal to be delayed,' Sam said.

Another strategy that Glide employed was to keep a careful note of why potential customers had failed to buy. It might be that they had expressed an interest, but were unable to buy at that time. Glide's sales team kept the details for these companies on file, and then found ways – when the time was right – to re-engage with the contacts, perhaps by inviting them to a corporate event Glide had organized.

It strikes me that knowing the right time may be an issue here – can you really time an event to fit with the buying pattern of a potential customer? Presumably the point is to have enough events running so that these potential customers will come when they are ready.

Another way that Glide maximized its opportunities to sell was by using information technology to capture its knowledge about potential clients and share this within the sales team. Sam told me he was very hot on getting staff to use the company's customer-relationship management system to note down what was discussed at client meetings. This enabled everyone in the business to keep up to date with relationships the business had, and to ensure that one team did not try to cover ground another had been over.

One of the challenges of adopting a client database is getting people to use the system to full effect. It only takes a few people in the team to resist it to render a new way of working redundant. At Glide, they attempted to overcome this potential pitfall by having weekly sales meetings, where all members of the sales team had to go through their particular sales pipelines. Pestering e-mails might be another way of achieving the same aim but it was not the style at Glide, Sam explained to me. Instead, the team meetings ensured that it was pretty obvious to all concerned if someone was not using the technology available.

When it came to technology use, Sam also led by example, writing a blog for the website from the chief executive. This was part of a wider social networking strategy, including a Twitter feed and Facebook page to share news with customers, all of which was in part at least aimed at lifting sales.

Sam admitted to me that the social networking commitment was a personal challenge because it meant stepping back from being a hands-on manager. Perhaps he was being forced to be less of a meddler in the business, which, as has already been noted in this book, is no bad thing.

Teamwork is key to sales

Sales processes can be further improved, by which I mean accelerated, by having members of a sales team that work together more often. This was a strategy employed by Fourth Hospitality, another web-based software provider I spoke to, this time specializing in human resources systems for the hospitality sector.

Salespeople are notoriously individualistic, so cooperation was not necessarily an easy option for Fourth Hospitality's sales director James England. However, he explained to me that putting sales executives into teams enabled the whole operation to function better. What this did was to encourage people to challenge each other's actions more often, which in turn gave them the confidence to drop certain leads that were not working and instead focus on the more productive ones.

'We don't incentivize people to say no,' James told me. 'It is simply a by-product of meeting and challenging each other to ask the right questions or qualify out the opportunity.'

One of the important workplace changes Fourth made that helped, according to James, was to encourage the sales teams to use web-based conferencing tools rather than face-to-face meetings with clients. The hit rate on new customer acquisitions can be very low, so every personal visit that does not pay off can be expensive in terms of petrol for a car journey or a rail or plane ticket, not to mention the opportunity cost of the time spent away from clients who actually do want to buy. Going virtual can therefore be a dramatic saving. In Fourth's case, this was a couple of thousand pounds a week per salesperson.

This is not to say that you can avoid human contact to build sales. Nothing could be further from the truth. For all James's belief in the power of technology, Fourth's sales team were also using the opportunities they had to get out and meet their clients. Given that these people worked in the hospitality sector, one assumes that there were plenty of opportunities to do this.

Good customer service can be a sales strategy

Although technology has many merits in terms of finding and managing new customers, there is something to be said for personal contact that should not be missed. The digital age has spawned an array of technologies to help entrepreneurs reach their customers, from Google adwords to corporate Facebook pages. However, for many, there is nothing to beat the old-school techniques of knocking on doors and getting recommendations for a job well done.

Good service is critical to all kinds of businesses, not just the obvious ones like retailers.

Rolls-Royce is a manufacturer of jet engines, but it actually makes a lot of its profit from servicing those parts so that they can continue operating at peak capacity for many years. It only takes one incident, such as the problems Qantas had with its Rolls-Royce engines in 2010, to undermine a hard-won reputation.

Scott and Lisa Sumner are passionate believers in the power of good customer service. The poor service provided by other companies was one of the main reasons that they got started, Scott told me. He explained how he had spent two 'miserable' years working for another cleaning company whose ethics, he said, left a great deal to be desired. It was Lisa who then encouraged him to set up his own company.

Their corporate cleaning business, Olivers Mill, grew into a £3 m turnover operation with more than 200 customers entirely on word-of-mouth recommendations. The staff headcount had reached 330 people when I met them in 2011 but, in 15 years of trading, the Kent-based company had never once hired a sales executive. Scott explained that he and Lisa did toy with the idea of building a sales team for their business. They spent £12,000 on a third-party telesales service, but stopped after it produced just three new client jobs.

Their success has been all the more remarkable because they started with no clients. It was made clear to Scott in no uncertain terms that he would not be able to poach any clients from his former employer. They also had just £30 in seed capital, Scott told me. As a result, they had to look to their own resources to drum up business. As has been mentioned earlier in this book, the support of friends and family (as well as fools) is the key to how most start-ups get off the ground. Olivers Mill, named after Scott and Lisa's first home together, was no exception, although the support came in the form of recommendations and contacts rather than financial capital.

Lisa's sister Emma provided them with Olivers Mill's first customers by advising her employer to use the service. As a result of their doing such a good job, that company then recommended Olivers Mill to other businesses and the client base just grew. There is something very enticing about the Sumners' way of doing business. A venture built on referrals is in many ways stronger because it has deeper relationships with its customer base.

However, it must be noted that their success has been helped by a good dose of good fortune as well as hard work in making every job count. Such a strategy also requires a certain way of working, not least in encouraging clients to recommend you to others. It is not human nature to do this all the time, after all.

In the case of Olivers Mill, the founders tried to practise what they preached by recommending customers to other people if the Sumners thought that the services they provided were worthwhile. Scott gave me the example of a language school Olivers Mill was looking at working with. He and Lisa actually saw some value for their own business from the service because many of their employees were not native English speakers. As a result they decided to set up a deal whereby they would subsidize language classes for their employees at the language school. The hope was that this in turn would encourage the language school to be generous in its comments about Olivers Mill.

This may not be considered normal business behaviour. But then again, acting out of character is a great way to get customers' attention. In the current age, where gadgets, social networking and new communications technologies seem to dominate our lives, the best way to act differently may be to return to more analogue techniques. It is a case of thinking how all your competitors talk to their customers and then doing something different. If you are a business rooted in technology, a website for instance, you might try sending handwritten notes via the snail mail. It will certainly get you noticed.

It is worthwhile remembering that physically being somewhere is still critical to most business growth, whether it is taking time to get on a plane and meet a person face to face or making sure you have a stall at the right trade shows. Time after time I am told how these kinds of trips, meeting people in person, make all the difference to a company's success.

A few sales tips

The thing about sales strategies is that there are lots of people willing to give you their personal pearls of wisdom.

Roger Harrop, an independent consultant and business adviser, told me that profitable sales growth is actually very easy to achieve by following a few simple rules. The first of these is only to sell to people who have money. Even in times of recession, Roger noted, there are still a lot of people doing very well. We spoke when economic conditions were still very difficult and yet he was able to make a list of 31 market sectors that were still growing.

Roger's next piece of advice was to make it as easy as possible for people to buy from you. At the heart of this point is a fact that many people often forget: that it is a lot cheaper and easier to sell more to existing customers than to spend time and money hunting for new ones. 'If someone bought 1,000 items from you a year ago, send them an e-mail with a pro forma invoice for another 1,000,' Roger told me.

'It won't work 100 per cent of the time, but it might work 40 per cent of the time.'

This is not to say that shortening the sales cycle is easy. Sam at Glide admitted to me that even with his company's successes, the sales process was still a constant struggle. We spoke when the UK economy was starting to pull itself out of recession, but he said that he was actually finding it tougher then to add new sales than when the overall economy had been contracting.

Beware of overtrading

So far we have discussed the sales function as if more sales are always a good thing. This may not be the case. One of the biggest risks to companies is not having too few sales, but having so many that it runs out of cash trying to service them. It is an issue with a name: overtrading. It is the reason why insolvency practitioners are usually at their busiest not when an economy is in a recession but when it is pulling out of the mire.

It may not be the sales team's fault that a company is at risk of overtrading. One of the key problems is getting the finance to pay for an increase in production. Here, the advice is to run a tight credit management operation, getting bills paid as quickly as possible, and make sure your financial planning is as rigorous as possible. It also helps to have good access to finance in these situations and the minimum of outstanding debt.

The problem of overtrading is also likely to be partly an issue of getting enough people to do the work. If your business needs specialist staff to operate, as in the case of a technology company in need of software engineers, it may not be able to hire enough new staff in time. Here it helps to think as much outside the box as possible. When skills are in short supply in your home market, it may help to have a team of employees abroad, where the supply of workers is more plentiful and cheaper to hire. In such circumstances, it may actually be your sales pipeline that can help you get through the problem.

Rather than trying to accelerate sales, this may be the moment to slow the process down. This is sometimes easier said than done, but it may be possible to use due diligence processes to manage the time it takes to bring a new customer on board. They may even appreciate your concern about ensuring that they are brought on board correctly.

One company that was able to do this was more2. Its clever consumer databases have enabled successful UK retailers like Links of London and White Stuff to better understand and sell to their customers. Attracting sales was not a problem for more2, but being able to service its new customers was a concern. In 2010, its revenue climbed 30 per cent to £5m and the sales team hit their annual target for client acquisition inside six months. However, the company struggled to meet demand because of the shortage of skilled engineers and account directors it needed to service new customers.

The advantage more2 had, however, was that its service was complex and implementing it could be time consuming, so it was relatively easy to manage clients' expectations of how long it would take to deliver. 'We never say we cannot take someone on, but there is a process of evaluating everyone's data,' Sanjay Patel, more2's commercial director, told me. 'People come on as fast as we want them to.'

Another fast-growing business that faced the risk of overtrading in its early days was Trade Mark Direct. Like other rebel entrepreneurs in this book, the founders of Trade Mark Direct have taken advantage of the efficiencies offered by the web to provide a long-established service more cheaply. In its case, this meant cutting out the fees for conventional patent attorneys to offer a cut-price trademark registration service. The results on the amount of business the company could attract were dramatic. In a little over two years after it started trading, Trade Mark Direct became one of the three largest patent firms in the UK in terms of the number of trademark applications it filed.

As a young company, it did not want to turn away business. However, it was struggling to cope with the increased demand. As with more2, the solution came in the form of managing demand.

In the case of Trade Mark Direct, the company could use its systems to make it a less interesting prospect for those only interested in making one application, the kinds of client that required the most amount of attention for the minimum reward. The changes needed were only small, and took little time to implement, but made managing new client leads easier. As a result, the company was able to deal with more inquiries while not stretching its resources too far.

Another way to avoid overtrading is to prepare in advance with the type of financing you use. For certain sectors, such as retail and the restaurant trade, invoice discounting can be a life saver here. Funds are released by the bank in return for customers' invoices so you can get working capital just when you need it.

The system does have downsides: it is not a workable solution for companies in all sectors and it can be an expensive way of obtaining finance because of the fees banks and other providers put upon the service. However, it is an avenue worth considering.

Squeezing the lemon

Conversations on sales inevitably revolve about getting new customers on board to increase your revenue. However, it is important to look at how existing customers can provide more revenue for your business, not least because this is usually a lot less expensive to do than new customer acquisition.

In recent years, a deep recession and uncertain recovery have forced lots of people to eke out more from their available resources. For entrepreneurs, this should be something they are used to doing. Waste not, want not, as the cliché goes.

Of course, getting customers to buy more requires a new set of strategies. Sarah Thewlis and Robert Graham, founders of Thewlis Graham Associates, an executive search business, told me how they were doing this in 2011. They launched their company using the clients they had gained at US headhunting firm Gundersen Partners after it decided to close its European business. At the time, 65 per cent of these clients gave Sarah and Robert one-off assignments. Six months later, 49 per cent of clients were repeat users.

'One of the difficulties of the executive search business is that you go in, do a job and move on,' Sarah told me. 'What we are trying to do is have a consulting relationship rather than something that is one-off.' Sarah and Robert were able to do this by bringing in outside help, paying an independent recruitment consultant to visit clients after an appointment had been made for what they call a 'post-audit review'. The aim of these sessions was to find out from the client and the successful candidate how the process went but, more importantly, what Thewlis Graham might be able to do for them in the future.

One metaphor I came across at Cranfield University that best describes this process is one of 'squeezing the lemon'. It is a cooking analogy, related to the common situation in which a recipe requires the cook to use the juice of half a lemon in the dish. Most people will slice a lemon in half, squeeze the liquid out of one half then discard the remaining flesh along with the other half of the fruit. After all, how often is it that you need a lemon in a recipe?

The point made by the staff at Cranfield is that you could probably get a lot more out of your lemon if only you tried. If you got a better lemon squeezer, you might get more juice out of the half of the lemon you actually used. Better still, if you organized your weekly meals a bit better, or had a bigger dinner party, you might not end up wasting the half of the lemon you threw away.

The lemon-squeezing analogy can apply to many different aspects of an ambitious business, but it works particularly well when thinking about getting more from existing customers. In a study by Cranfield it was calculated that up to 90 per cent of businesses that achieve sustainable profitable growth do so by selling more to existing customers or organizations, and to others that were like them.

In its Business Growth and Development Programme for ambitious owners of established businesses, Cranfield's staff encourage the development of lemon-squeezing workshops to find new ways to sell to existing customers. It sometimes helps to offer a prize to staff who come up with the best lemon-squeezing idea.

There are examples of this kind of behaviour in many of the world's most impressive companies. Ryanair, which I have already alluded to several times for its rebel entrepreneur credentials, does this all the time by getting people to pay for things that other airlines might offer for free. It is not just the sandwiches that you buy because there is no in-flight meal. Scratch cards have been a huge success for the company. These items are sold by Ryanair cabin crew, which means that people who would normally be a pure cost to the company have become in effect the airline's sales staff, generating revenue for the business in the process.

Opportunity is never far away

In times of economic downturn, as we have been stuck in over recent years, it is often not simply a case of adding sales, but of keeping your existing customers. This can be particularly important during recessions, when customers may ditch your business in an effort to fight costs.

I explained in Chapter 6 how Etc Venues, Wilson Sherriff and Systems Associates reacted to a drop in spending by their customers by finding new opportunities for their businesses. These stories can offer a lesson here in terms of looking for new clients to sell to. In many ways, what happened to these companies is what happens to every business at some point wherever they are in the world: the market changes and they need to refocus their selling efforts on new opportunities.

Again it is about the importance of being able to pivot and adjust your business model accordingly.

The conclusion

In terms of the lessons of selling offered by this chapter, there are several points to remember.

The first, in finding good sales staff, is to hire for attitude and then train on the job.

Outside help can be useful when looking for good salespeople, but it is important to remember that it is always going to be difficult to find this particular type of person for your business.

Some businesses actually do without sales teams by getting their customers to refer them. However, cases where you are going to be able to do this are likely to be rare.

Accelerating sales is about making sure you know the right people: the ones who make the buying decisions. It is highly unlikely that there will only be one person involved in the buying process.

When times are tough it may help to remember that there are always people you can sell to, even in hard times, but you need to make it as easy as possible for these people to buy from you.

Remember that the best way to increase your sales may be to 'squeeze the lemon' and get your existing customers to buy more from you. The best opportunities, and certainly the cheapest to grab, are often those that are already nearest to you.

Even if people do not choose to buy from you they may do so in the future, so if people express an interest in what you are selling it is worth making a record of their details and keeping in contact with them.

Technology may be useful in the selling process, for example in sharing information on potential sales leads, but never forget the human factor because people ultimately buy from people.

Finally, remember that, important as it is to increase sales, it is vital that you have the resources to satisfy them without running out of cash. Overtrading is a real danger for fast-growing companies, so make sure you have the financial and operational support, and if possible manage your demand.

Chapter Eight
Failure is not
failure if you learn

One of the implicit problems with writing a self-help book, as this one might be perceived to be, is the assumption that following any of the guidance given within its pages will guarantee success. If only life were so simple.

One of the core principles of this book is that rebel entrepreneurs are a rare breed. One of the main reasons for this is the high failure rate among all start-ups. A study in the UK, for example, found that, for every 100 VAT-registered businesses set up in 1995, only 32 were still registered in 2005. (And among small new companies that are not registered for VAT the failure rate is much higher, as mentioned in the Prologue.)

Not only do most new businesses close within a decade of starting, even those that succeed often do not grow very much, and many go through periods of decline. A study of the business population of New Zealand for the Ministry of Economic Development in Wellington found that between 2000 and 2005, only 8 per cent of companies increased their sales, while 40 per cent remained stable, 30 per cent ceased trading and 22 per cent shrank.

Just to reiterate, this means that not only did just a tiny fraction of the total actually grow, but over half of the sample either lost sales or disappeared completely. Also, more than three times as many companies shrank as grew. These kinds of figures are repeated for countries across the world.

Julian Frankish, a senior economist at Barclays Bank, studied the data on new business creation in England and Wales covering 5,800 start-ups over a three-year period. He found that in each six-month period up to three years, a surviving new business had a 53 per cent chance of growing and a 47 per cent chance of declining. Moreover, he found that growth in one six-month period had almost no influence on increases or decreases in the following six months. Approximately half of the businesses he studied ceased trading within four years of start-up. Closure rates peaked at about 12 to 18 months.

What Mr Frankish's research shows is that growth is the least likely outcome of any start-up, and continuous growth is truly exceptional. This is a sobering finding.

One of the great joys about writing about entrepreneurs is their seemingly limitless confidence in their own ability to turn adversity into opportunity. The flip side of this, however, may be that founders find it difficult to deal with adversity. This should not be the case.

The point of this chapter is to discuss the random nature of life, which means that all successful entrepreneurship to some extent involves a degree of luck.

At the same time, however, it is nigh impossible for any entrepreneur to get anywhere without also facing a degree of misfortune. The point I will try to get across is that long-term success relies on your using your bad luck to positive effect. This could mean learning from the pain to make you better prepared in the future. It could mean just picking yourself up and getting back into the game. Marc Andreessen, the co-founder of Netscape, summed up this approach nicely in a blog post in which he said chance favours those who have a bias for action and strong sense of curiosity.

The problem for many entrepreneurs may be the fact that they are positive people by nature, so tend not to want to discuss the downside of start-up activity. While many entrepreneurs have experienced a business that goes under, few, I have found, want to talk about it in a public forum even though they know that this is the way they have learnt lessons from others.

This issue of failure is an interesting one because it is so often presented as a negative, a sort of cancer killing good companies. However, it is also a Darwinian process in which entrepreneurs can be made stronger by picking themselves up and trying again.

The word failure may not even be the right term for this process of companies folding. It may be that the owner simply realized that there was a better proposition elsewhere. Indeed, that second venture, with the benefit of additional experience, may be the making of the entrepreneur involved. If they had not 'failed' once, they would never have succeeded with what ultimately turned out to be a much bigger, more lucrative idea. It might also be that the person who founded the 'failed' business decided entrepreneurship was not his or her bag.

This does not mean that the founder necessarily lost everything he or she had in the process – what many may understand as failure. Indeed, the person involved, who took a considerable risk in going it alone, may have gained skills they could apply to a salaried job. Such people may not become rebel entrepreneurs in the sense that we have looked at it throughout this book, but they have not 'failed' if they have learnt something from the process of founding a business.

This chapter is about looking at failure in a positive way. It is the idea that a few missteps can give you an understanding that you would never have achieved if the path of life had been smooth and always moving forward. In that sense it may even appeal to the kind of glass-half-full entrepreneur, who hates to consider the downside of anything.

To do this, I will share a few examples of stories people have told me about the difficulties they have had as entrepreneurs. The point here is to illustrate that failure is not always the end, but can be a necessary experience for development as an entrepreneur.

These stories are precious because I know they are so difficult for people to share. When people start opening up, they then hear from others about how the same shocking experiences happened to them.

This is one of the reasons why entrepreneurs like to join networking clubs like The Supper Club, mentioned in Chapter 3, which runs private dinners in which founders can talk openly about issues, secure in the knowledge that what they say will not be repeated outside. 'What is said in the room, stays in the room,' is the mantra of Supper Club founder Duncan Cheatle.

Someone who is passionate about the fact that entrepreneurs can find success out of failure is Luke Johnson, a serial founder who now runs private equity firm Risk Capital Partners as well as writing a column for the *Financial Times*. 'No one said hitting the jackpot was easy; but then, if it was, it wouldn't be any fun,' he wrote in one of his columns in 2011.

I hope I have made clear that failure is not necessarily a problem. Fear of failure, however, can be.

The most comprehensive study into early-stage start-up activity around the planet is the Global Entrepreneurship Monitor (GEM). This annual report is completed by a global network of teams of academics, who specialize in entrepreneurial studies, spread across four continents. The complete study is overseen by Babson College, based in Wellesley, Massachusetts, which is a leading institution for the teaching of entrepreneurial management.

These people know what they are talking about when it comes to entrepreneurial behaviour. So it is telling that one of the key measures the GEM survey comes back to year after year as a way of telling whether countries have a greater or lesser propensity to create new businesses is the fear of failure among the local population. In the 2010 study, Greece had by far the highest score on GEM's fear of failure index. It is perhaps not surprising, then, that it was also the country least likely to have adults involved in start-up activity.

GEM's research indicates that failure in itself is not the reason people do not start a business, but the paralyzing worry among people that it may happen to them. As Franklin Roosevelt said: 'The only thing we have to fear is fear itself.'

Why the fear of failure can be so damaging

In talking about the problems of fear of failure, I am not talking about the need to keep your wits about you. Andy Grove, co-founder of Intel, made famous the phrase: 'Only the paranoid survive.' It is one that has served many entrepreneurs well. What is a problem is the inability to embrace the fact that things sometimes do not work out as planned. Aligned to this is the fact that failure to grab the opportunity to learn when fate deals you a bad hand or you just slip up may well destine you as a founder to a life of mediocrity rather than becoming a rebel entrepreneur.

So what do I mean by fear of failure, and why is that so wrong? GEM points out that the fundamental problem with the fear of failure is the way it prevents people from taking risks. It notes that developed countries whose citizens display the lowest fear of failure, such as the United States, Switzerland and the Netherlands, also tend to have the most innovation-driven economies. GEM also finds an inverse relationship between the level of fear of failure that citizens of a country display and the degree to which people see good opportunities to start a business. Reduce the fear of failure, GEM's researchers conclude, and you may well see more people find a reason to start up a new venture.

So how do you shake off the fear of failure? After all it is an entirely understandable emotion to possess. It is utterly human to be concerned about venturing beyond the world you know in case of danger lurking in the shadows. The urge to fear failure seems to get worse the older, richer and more settled you become, according to GEM. Young people do not have families and mortgages to support, and immigrants may well be shut out from the better-paid jobs that go to people who already have the connections to employment. While these factors alone do not on their own create an entrepreneur – indeed there may be others, such as a lack of support networks to get started that work against young people and migrants – they suggest that having less to lose is a key factor in overcoming fear of failure.

It is difficult to see how you engineer that when you are older, and have become used to being in one place your entire life. However, many do. The average age for starting a business in the UK, for instance, is 35 to 45, according to GEM.

It may be that you consider the option of *not* trying to start a business is worse than playing it safe. Before the financial crisis, some very successful entrepreneurs took the plunge from what were seen as very safe jobs partly for this reason. A classic example of this would be the founders of smoothie maker Innocent Drinks, Richard Reed, Adam Balon and Jon Wright. At the time that they set up the business they all had well-paid, relatively secure salaried jobs in consulting and advertising. I have already explained the story about how they decided whether to take a risk of starting Innocent with the bins at the music festival. It was a risk, but these were also relatively young, well-qualified men, who could probably have got another salaried role if Innocent hadn't worked out. So perhaps they fitted into GEM's analysis of the risk-taking youth.

More often, however, the decision to go it alone is forced upon the founder. In times of severe economic hardship, like the ones the world has been going through in recent years, the redundancy-cheque start-up is one of the most common scenarios.

Again, the point is to look at this in a positive way. After all, if this is your lot, you are in good company. Steve Jobs made this point in his now famous address to students at Stanford University. It was only because he was pushed out of Apple that he ended up taking control of the animation studio Pixar, which he later sold to Disney in a deal valuing the business at $7.4 bn.

Few may say it at the time, but many rebel entrepreneurs I have met have concurred with this sentiment, noting years after that first frightening start that losing the salaried job was the best thing that happened to them.

Failure can be your own stupid fault

Of course, there are also many instances where failure has been brought upon the company as a result of the founder's own stupid decisions, or the limitations of the person's abilities.

Here are a few examples of how you can be the master of your own failure.

Common mistake 1: treating the bank like a cashpoint

There might well have been a problem with maintaining the basics of company management, such as ensuring that the business always has enough cash to keep it functioning – many forget that businesses do not die because of a lack of sales but because the cash runs out.

As I noted in Chapter 1, on several occasions in the last few (difficult) years I have been phoned by desperate company owners trying to find someone in the media who will tell their story of how the bank has brought in the insolvency practitioners to wind up the business. Although some of these are genuine stories of banking incompetence, where the owners themselves are no doubt victims, these are outweighed by others where, once a little digging has been undertaken into the surroundings of the closure, you get a strong sense that the business owner himself (and it usually is a he) could have prevented the situation from escalating by communicating a bit more with those who hold the purse strings.

This is not a scientific sample, not least because only certain people will pick up the phone and try to get through to a journalist. However, there is no doubt that there have been many cases, particularly in recent years, where failure in cash management has been as much a problem of company owners not talking to their banks as it has been of evil bankers turning over customers.

Problems often arise with the bank because of a lack of regular communication with the account manager. It is wise to schedule monthly meetings with this person even when things are going well – in fact especially when things are going well – just to keep him or her updated on sales for the quarter, monthly expenses and the state of the market. Do this in the good times, and it might not come as such a shock to the bank manager when you have to come begging for finance when the business gets hit with a sudden shortfall in cash.

Although the banking industry has many problems and a lot of things to answer for in its treatment of small businesses over the last few years, it cannot be blamed for being unable to help a company it has heard little about.

The bank may well have been foolish in lending money to a particular business in the first place if it based its opinion on the price of the owner's property, under which many loans were secured – at least until the 2008 banking crisis struck. However, if the business owner wanted to make the bank understand the basic viability of the start-up plan, he or she should have shown the bank the numbers that proved this when the founder first applied for finance.

Some of those who have been failures in the financial crisis have at least in part been the authors of their own downfall because they did not follow this one very basic rule of good business administration.

Common mistake 2: putting your eggs in one basket

One of the biggest risks to an ambitious growing business is becoming too reliant on a single customer. But, in spite of the warnings about the dangers of putting all your eggs in one basket, many founders still find themselves in this position.

This was what happened to an entrepreneur I met called Mark Needham and his business Widget UK, which distributed consumer electronics products. He was lucky, however. In 2006, Widget lost £10m of its £23.4m annual sales after the withdrawal of a single contract to supply GPS navigational devices to Comet, a bricks-and-mortar electrical retailer that at the time dominated the British high street and out-of-town shopping malls.

Such a loss could have been game-over for a relatively small player like Widget, but Mark acted fast and fortunately found an escape route for his business. 'We asked ourselves which part of the market was growing fastest,' he told me. 'The answer was e-commerce players.'

Mark's sales team started hitting the phones, calling all of the largest players in online consumer electronics, such as Amazon.co.uk, the British arm of the global internet department store, eBuyer and Dabs.com. They not only found willing customers. Mark's team was so successful in attracting new business from the virtual shopping outlets that Widget's sales for the following year actually increased – even with the loss of the Comet contract. 'There is little alternative to gritting your teeth and trying harder,' Mark told me in classic rebel entrepreneur style.

At the time Widget was a small, relatively young player, which helped enormously because there were not the layers of management or people who had got used to selling in a certain way and come to resist the sudden need for change.

As has been said before, it is easier to face failure if you are young. The same is true if you are a young company. At the time, Widget only employed 20 people. As I noted in the hero chapter, when a company is this size the charisma of a founder can still motivate the entire workforce to make radical changes to their routines. That was exactly what Widget needed to do. 'We were in a position to act immediately if an e-commerce player phoned and asked for a particular item,' Mark told me.

He was lucky to have a small, young business, an idea about how to solve his problem and, perhaps most importantly, the luck of finding companies willing to give Widget a break.

Others are not so lucky. For all the success stories like Widget, there are many more companies that do not survive the external shocks. If you are still breathing, however, Widget shows it can be worth continuing the fight, if you can face up to that fear of failure.

The uncomfortable truth for anyone embarking on the entre-preneurial journey is that there is no guaranteed route to success. Whatever you do as a founder to create the perfect company, there will be crises ahead that have never happened in quite the same way before and could well be fatal to the enterprise you have worked so hard to build. Risk does not go away just because you have survived longer than anyone else. In fact the risks may increase because you have become set in your ways.

Hard work is always essential to success. But often luck, or rather bad luck, plays a considerable role too.

Life can be cruel so you have to deal with it

It is worth remembering as a founder that there are many things in life you just cannot control. It might be the development of a new technology that renders an important part of your business model obsolete. This has been happening in a dramatic way to many industries with the advent of the internet, from high-street shops to traditional media outlets. It might be the death of a key executive, or a change within a key customer, such as Widget experienced, that means it does not want your product or service. These are problems that are almost impossible to identify in advance and are not easy to solve because they are things that by their nature have never happened in quite the same way before.

Entrepreneurs, being optimists and overachievers by nature, often struggle to acknowledge in public that they have fallen victim to bad luck, because they would much rather pin the blame on a particular thing. They may find it particularly hard when events appear to conspire against them, perhaps because they are so used to feeling in control of their own destiny.

Bankruptcy, loss of revenue and breakdowns in business relationships are far more common than many company founders, and indeed small-business journalists, seem ready to admit. Sometimes the consequences can be devastating for the founders' personal lives as well as the business they were so keen to protect.

Take the case of Susie Willis, who co-founded the ethical baby-food business Plum Baby, who was asked to fire her partner in an eleventh-hour offer to save what had already become a troubled business. This was a difficult enough decision, but the man Susie had been asked to dispatch also happened to be her husband, Patrick. This might appear to be about the worst situation a founder could face, but it was made even harder by the timing of the announcement. The call from the board saying it wanted Susie to break the news to her husband came as the couple were on a family holiday in Cornwall, taking a rare week away from the business they had worked so hard to create. 'It was miserable,' she recalled to me shortly afterwards. 'The gun was on the table.'

Susie is nothing if not brave. Despite the appalling task she had been given, she accepted the ultimatum and Patrick was told to depart by the woman with whom he had started a business, married and produced three children. Patrick subsequently took up the post of managing director at Node Explore, a technology start-up funded by one of the private equity firms that he and Susie had met while seeking funds for Plum Baby. However, the stress took its toll and shortly afterwards the couple separated.

It could be argued that the path to this crisis point could have been avoided, but it was hard to see how at the time. Indeed, in the first four years after its creation in 2004, Plum Baby had been doing all the right things, it seemed to Patrick and Susie. The business had achieved great success in attracting customers, a notoriously difficult element for any new product business. As a result of hard pitching to the buyers employed by the main retailers, Plum Baby's quinoa-based foods were on the shelves of most of the UK's leading supermarket chains. Turnover had grown quickly, reaching £3.5 m by the company's third year, enabling the business to become the sixth most popular brand in the baby-food category by UK retail analysts.

With hindsight, it was obvious that these early successes helped create the conditions for the troubles that were to batter Plum Baby later on. The company became reliant on certain businesses and did not have a back-up plan. To be fair, there was no reason for Patrick and Susie to believe that they needed one. With the orders coming in thick and fast, Plum Baby's manufacturer, a small French family-owned business, was unable to produce the amounts promised, creating stock shortages and undermining future sales. 'When you are a small business, that really hurts,' Susie explained. 'It made the everyday cash situation incredibly tight.'

Susie and Patrick had already remortgaged their house to help finance the business. Like many owners, as we have already noted in this book, the Willises' had also borrowed money from family and friends to get the business off the ground. However, the cash crisis caused by the inability to satisfy the escalating sales meant that the business got to a point where it was going to run out of money in a matter of weeks. Susie described it as a 'hand-to-mouth existence'.

Some of the Willises' troubles could be attributed to the character of the individuals involved. Susie seemed personally aware of this when she related the story to me. She recalled how, after spending a particularly long period of time and effort gathering 15 syndicates to talk about an investment to support the company's growth, she stormed out of the meeting that had been arranged with them, mortified by what she considered was their low valuation of the business. 'I remember my husband cupping his head in his hands, saying, "you have done it again, Susie,"' she said.

However, the trouble with the idea that could not have been prevented was that there were also many outside factors. Although Plum Baby's crisis period happened before the financial crisis of 2008, when many small businesses saw their credit lines evaporate, the banks it went to said they were unwilling to lend to a business that had yet to break even. As a result, the Willises approached potential venture capital backers with the intention of raising £2 m and reducing their stake from a majority holding to 30 per cent.

The couple spent three months doing nothing else but fund raising and keeping their heads above water. This furious activity meant that they could continue to pay all their suppliers, but they had to rely on a great deal of goodwill from their logistical support provider, which was also a shareholder in the business. Susie, who became creative director of Plum Baby after the board let Patrick go, was always full of praise for her partner, whom she described to me as a 'multi-talented' man.

The business also came through this rough period and achieved an exit for the investors. In May 2010, Plum Baby was bought by the venture capital firm Darwin Private Equity for £10 m. At the time it was on track to generate annual revenue of £15 m.

Many other businesses are not even this lucky. A crisis happens and the business does not survive. However, it is also important to remember that failure has also happened to some of the most celebrated entrepreneurs, who then went on to achieve remarkable success.

I mentioned how Steve Jobs led the sale of Pixar to Disney. Well, Disney itself is a story of failure followed by success. In 1922, at the age of 22, Walt Disney founded his first company Laugh-O-gram Films. He had raised $15,000 (about $190,000 in today's money) from private investors to fund a new animation business, based in Kansas. The young Mr Disney used this cash to rent space in a new development and hired a team of staff to produce his films.

He had some early success, winning an $11,100 contract from another small business, Pictorial Clubs, to distribute the cartoons his company made. Mr Disney took a $100 down payment for the cartoons, but six months later Pictorial Clubs went bankrupt. Since Mr Disney was no longer able to pay the rent or the wages owed to his staff, he borrowed another $2,000 against his film equipment and materials from one of his original investors. However, it was still not enough. A year later, Mr Disney was declared bankrupt, owing money to his former employees and investors.

Of course, this was not the end of the story for this determined entrepreneur. By the time he was declared a bankrupt, Mr Disney was already on his way to Los Angeles, where he would use his second chance to build what would become one of the world's most powerful media companies.

Despite these tales of business comebacks, however, insolvency remains a dirty word in many parts of the world. This only contributes to the problem of fear of failure. In the United States, there were 1,117,771 bankruptcy filings in 2008. Of those, 744,424 were Chapter 7 bankruptcies, where the owners' non-exempt property was sold, while 362,762 were Chapter 13, a voluntary arrangement by the debtor in which an attempt is made to reorganize the business and get it trading again.

By any measure, this is a significant amount of failure. However, the US bankruptcy system is heavily weighted towards turning failure into success. There are two kinds of legal bankruptcy under US law: involuntary, when one or more creditors petition to have a debtor judged insolvent by a court, and voluntary, when the debtor brings the petition. In both cases, the objective is an orderly and equitable settlement of obligations. More importantly, many companies do come through the other side.

The 1978 Bankruptcy Reform Act removed some of the rigidities of the old law and permitted more flexibility in procedures. Although the 1984 Bankruptcy Reform Act curtailed some of the more liberal provisions of the earlier legislation, it remains a critical support for troubled companies to get back on their feet.

Perhaps the most famous element of the legislation is Chapter 11, which deals with the reorganization of businesses. It provides that, unless the court rules otherwise, the company's owners (the debtors) remain in possession of the business and in control of its operation. They and their creditors are then allowed considerable flexibility to resolve the company's problems. For instance, the company can secure financing and loans on favourable terms by giving new lenders first priority on any future earnings. The court may also permit the company to reject and cancel contracts. The debtor is also protected from other litigation against the business through the imposition of what is called an 'automatic stay', which requires all creditors to cease attempts to collect money owed to them.

Although Chapter 11 protection can be used as a mechanism for liquidation of a business, it has been a life saver for many US companies. As I was finishing this book, American Airlines became the latest large US corporate to seek the sanctuary of Chapter 11 protection. The airline industry has been a particularly frequent user of Chapter 11 protection. In 2006, it was calculated that over half the industry's seating capacity was on airlines that were in Chapter 11. What it enabled these companies to do was to reorganize themselves so they could recover, which most of them have done.

This is not to say that entering Chapter 11 is a badge of honour for a company. Quite the reverse. A filing for Chapter 11 protection has also been the final death rattle for many giant US companies, which have subsequently been broken up or sold on to other companies. But the fact that there are Chapter 11 protections is a sign of a society that can give second chances to companies.

The morals of this can be questioned, but what it does seem to do is to ensure at least some good comes out of a bad situation. It also seems to go hand in hand with the US attitude to failure and giving people second chances. That goes part of the way to explaining why the United States consistently tops GEM's survey of the most entrepreneurial nations based on start-up activity. It is also why other countries, such as Australia, have changed their bankruptcy rules to mirror some of what Chapter 11 protection achieves.

The fear of failure, and the feeling that it is something only bad entrepreneurs go through, is often only part of the reason why founders tend to keep quiet about it when they go through some form of bankruptcy protection. Owners are likely to face the wrath of disappointed customers, unpaid suppliers, employees who lose their livelihoods and investors whose money is wiped out. For founders, who are naturally positive people, this can be hard to accept. But it should not be a reason for defeat. How you react to failure can be the difference between whether you are finally a success or not.

Doug Richard, an American entrepreneur who now lives in the English university city of Cambridge, is a critic of the fear of failure in his adopted homeland, where he now provides advice to others wishing to start up on their own. In his secondary school in the United States, he recalled to me, pupils were taught to expect to have to make 100 sales calls before having a success. Later in life, when he was trying to start a business, he would remember this teaching every time someone he hoped would be a customer turned him down. He claimed that he would celebrate this 'failure' because the lesson from his school days was that it meant he was one step closer to getting that successful deal.

Mark Suster, a founder of two start-ups who is now a partner in San Francisco-based venture capital firm GRP Partners, talks on his blog about having to make 50 phone calls in order to get anything done in life, whether that is a venture capital firm trying to land a deal, a new company trying to get a customer, or even a journalist trying to get a story.

These kinds of theories, and there are many in the United States, give the impression that individuals can do something about their destiny.

However, it is also important to remember as an entrepreneur that life is a bit random.

The random nature of entrepreneurial success

Professor David Storey at Sussex University compares the lot of entrepreneurs to the economic theory of the gambler's ruin, suggesting that running a business is like being at a roulette table. The business owner, like the gambler, is faced by a risky proposition and has to make a decision, in Professor Storey's analogy. Owners can either use their resources (chips) to gamble on getting a successful outcome (breaking the casino's bank), or close the business (take their earnings away from the roulette table).

Business owners who decide to play the game have to decide how much they want to gamble and when. Having made this decision they may be lucky and win, so enhancing their stock of wealth and possibly making them more confident about the accuracy of their judgement, or they may lose. Failure may make them quit, but if they continue to gamble and lose, they will eventually be ruined because they have nothing more to play with and cannot get any further credit.

The theory of gambler's ruin is used by economists to explain why 'the house always wins' because a casino, with more resources at its disposal, can always afford to play for longer than any individual gambler. In business it helps to explain why many entrepreneurs end up in trouble because they do not have the ability to quit when they are ahead. This is not to say that entrepreneurs are reckless. It is just that decision making will always be imprecise when the person concerned has imperfect information to hand.

Only after the event can you see whether it would have made more sense to have taken what you had and get out of the game before disaster struck.

Remember, it may be second time unlucky

It could be said that entrepreneurs who have not failed are either unsuccessful, liars or not experienced enough.

For an example of the third case, you only have to look at those founders who have had a great first idea only to be followed by what music journalists call 'the difficult second album'. David Giampaolo, who runs Pi Capital, the London-based investor network for wealthy individuals, has seen a lot of founders in his time, many of whom could be described as rebel entrepreneurs. He told me the case of a man he knew who had built a very successful business, making a fortune upon its sale. After a while spent relaxing and enjoying his newfound wealth he decided to try it again, but the second idea proved a flop. He tried something else, which was equally unsuccessful. After the fourth failed attempt, during which he lost a large slice of his amassed fortune, the entrepreneur decided to return to what he had done in the first place that made him his money. 'Prior success is not proxy for future success,' David said. 'It helps, but it is no guarantee.'

Some of the second-time failures David has seen were not a million miles from their founders' original idea. However, the subsequent versions clearly lacked the element that made the original business concept a success. It is far from certain whether even doing what was originally done would result in another success, however, given the random nature of creating a business, according to David. Having said that, he told me he always preferred people who had another go.

David knows what he is talking about having been involved in hundreds of deals over many years. 'The worst thing is an entrepreneur who thinks that their success comes from hard work,' he told me. 'If I don't see humility and an appreciation of luck, chance and randomness, then I won't invest.'

Perhaps fewer people would be crippled by fear of failure if they knew the truth that even bankruptcy does not always mean the end for a determined founder, as Walt Disney showed.

Failure may also not even mean bankruptcy and material impoverishment. As I said at the beginning of this chapter, many businesses are closed not because they cannot trade, but just because the founders realized that the idea was not working to their satisfaction and they wanted to do something else, or perhaps move to the safety of a salaried post. The official survival statistics also fail to account for businesses that are sold, hardly a 'failed' outcome.

The business failure statistics should also reassure those who feel that they are the only ones that have not been able to make an idea work.

This random nature of business would not be a problem if more people involved in starting businesses admitted its existence.

The problem with most entrepreneurs is that they only talk to the public about their success stories. What business journalists then do is try to extrapolate from these stories the reasons for that company's success. The problem with this kind of analysis is that it at best only tells us the lessons from one company's history, which, as the academics tell us, is highly unlikely to be ever repeated again.

We need another explanation of business success that gives us a better understanding of how start-ups work. Sussex University's David Storey has done this. He calls it 'optimism and chance' (OC) theory. 'We see entrepreneurship as akin to a chance event, such as purchasing a lottery ticket or gambling at a roulette wheel in a casino,' he told me. 'Taking the lottery example, entrepreneurs can be compared with individuals who buy tickets for a low price, with a low possibility of winning any prize, and a very low probability of winning a large prize. However, to be eligible for a prize, the individual has to buy a ticket.' The random nature of success is something that most people who have never started a business talk about. What David introduces into the mix is one of the essential characteristics of entrepreneurs: the optimist belief that they are different from everyone else.

This combination of optimism and chance in OC theory explains the difference between, say, the level of successful start-ups in the United States compared with Europe. It is not that Europeans are more incompetent business builders; it is just that the perceived cost of starting a business in terms of what they must risk is seen to be higher. It is not just that Europeans may miss the security of a job protected by more employment law than in the United States. It is also that reputation is hard won and easily lost in Europe.

What OC theory also does is raise the prospect that there is no explanation of why firms that have grown either stop growing or decline. What we need in order to be better entrepreneurs is, therefore, a greater degree of humility about what we can learn as we become more experienced. Another way of looking at this, however, is that you often make your own luck by having a go.

Remember, the darkest moment is before the dawn

It was Samuel Goldwyn, the American film producer, who said: 'The harder I work, the luckier I become.' This has been proved time and time again among people we assume to have been prodigies, who in fact put in long hours, suffering many setbacks, in order to achieve their success.

The chic pink headquarters of H Forman & Sons in the recently scrubbed banks of the River Lee, overlooking the 2012 Olympic Park in London's East End, looks like a prime example of the kind of success the modern games were created to display. Lance Forman, the current owner of the fourth-generation family business, is certainly a formidable entrepreneur, not only ensuring that the art of salmon smoking remains in the East End, where it was introduced by the immigrant Jewish population over 100 years ago, but making improvements such as introducing a catering arm and a restaurant on site to serve the rapidly gentrifying local community.

There is little doubt that the current success of Formans is down to the smart thinking and hard work of the latest Mr Forman to shepherd the business. While other East End salmon smokeries went to the wall in the face of price competition with operations in Scotland and elsewhere, Formans focused on becoming a premium product, sold to many of the UK's finest restaurants, and charging a premium price as a result.

However, the company is also a world away from where it was when Lance took over. He tells of a conversation he had with the former managing director of Formans when he was considering the company's future. 'He said, "Lance, there is no future in this business because salmon is becoming a commodity. But don't worry, I will manage the decline for the family." I said, hang on, something is wrong here.'

For all Lance's considerable achievements, however, he has also been hit by a run of bad luck, with several near fatal events that were completely out of his hands. Indeed, there have been occasions in recent years when Formans could have disappeared entirely. The first came shortly after Lance took over the reins of the business in 1998: the smoking plant his father had built from scratch barely two decades earlier caught fire and was badly damaged. After struggling for six months in the remains of the building, Lance paid for the entire structure to be refurbished. Then in 2000, the River Lee overflowed and put the factory under three feet of water, contaminating it.

Such bad luck might have destroyed a lesser person, but Lance appeared determined to use each setback to take the business forward another step. When the factory burnt down, he made sure the £3 m replacement had a more efficient production flow. He also added a chef-training business and created Forman & Field, a fine-food delivery service championing British food from independent family farmers. When the flood soaked the new salmon smoking factory, Lance struck a deal with the UK government's health and safety officials to keep the place operating by proving that staff would sanitize every wall each day. 'For each disaster, you also have to find how can you use this to your advantage,' he told me.

Perhaps the most remarkable thing was that, during all this time of tumult, Formans did not miss a single day of deliveries, according to Lance. 'However big your problems are, the customer is not interested. They need your service.'

Other entrepreneurs are not as lucky as Lance. He is well aware of this in his local community, in which a hundred or so small businesses were dislodged by the compulsory purchase of land to build the venues for the 2012 Olympics. Many of those businesses have gone forever, Lance lamented to me. Preparing for the arrival of a major sporting event is not something often covered in business growth guides. It is difficult to understand how an entrepreneur could prepare for such an occurrence.

What Lance's story shows is that growing a successful business is often not a matter of luck coming your way, but of having the tenacity and drive to get back into the office and find a new business strategy if and when disaster strikes.

This is happening all the time among small businesses, where disruptions that often do not even register on local news can have a massive impact on their operations. Unlike large companies, which have whole departments to deal with disaster management, small businesses are buffeted by even quite small changes in their markets.

Insolvency is often not the end

Imagine the problems you would face if you had built your business on the idea that you act with integrity, only to be hit with a cash crisis that left you in danger of trading insolvently. This was what happened to Alex Cheatle. In 2003, his concierge business, Ten, ran into problems and found it could not settle its bills. 'We wanted to be the most trusted people,' Alex told me. However, the business, after an aggressive expansion during the dotcom boom years, was losing significant amounts of money. The final straw came when a potential investor pulled out and the company was at risk of trading insolvently.

Alex could have given up, but he was determined not to allow the company he had worked so hard to build go under. His solution was to create another limited liability company that could buy the assets of the old business, using a process in UK bankruptcy law called a creditors' voluntary liquidation. The rules would have allowed Alex to keep all the equity in the new business to himself, but he explained to me that he wanted to use this extremely difficult time to show goodwill to those who had backed him so far. As a result, he elected to give all his old investors shares in the new business, called Ten Lifestyle Management. 'If you are serious about being in the business of trust, you have to keep your integrity,' Alex told me. This was clearly important to Alex, who admitted to me that he had wanted to be an entrepreneur from an early age, having set up his first business ventures while still at school.

When it comes to insolvency, however, some people always lose out and this was certainly the case with Ten, not least when it came to the taxman. Although Alex told me that he was able to more than compensate all his suppliers once the new business was up and running, he had to admit that he never paid a penny of the bill owing to HM Revenue and Customs (HMRC). He defended his actions to me by noting that the new Ten, which in 2008 made a net profit of £404,000 on a £10.1m turnover, generated enough profit to pay HMRC many times what it owed the UK government in 2003.

There was also a price to be paid in jobs. When the original Ten was declared insolvent, Alex decided he had to cut the jobs of 26 people, or about half his payroll. This did not create a pleasant atmosphere. One of those made redundant sued for unfair dismissal. 'I had to make two more people redundant because of the settlement with her,' Alex explained. 'That made me upset.' He defended the decision to sacrifice people's jobs in order to save the business by noting that Ten subsequently grew to a workforce of 200, including several of the people he had had to dismiss six years earlier. 'I think people understood what we were having to do,' he told me.

This kind of behaviour towards people whose livelihoods depended upon Ten might be questioned by some of those affected. Paul Stanley, managing partner at Begbies Traynor, an insolvency specialist, explained to me that he sees the kind of arrangement used for Ten a lot, although not as much as the more controversial UK practice of pre-packaged, or phoenix, deals, where a buyer is found before the company enters administration and creditors are often left out of pocket. 'I understand why creditors feel miffed when someone puts a business down and buys it back,' he said. There is also a cost to society of insolvency procedures like this. Money that bankrupt companies cannot pay to the taxman is a drain on the public purse, which makes it harder to find the resources to pay for nurses and teachers.

After talking to Alex, I spoke to some of his investors. They at least were pleased with what he had done for them. Rupert Eastwood, an entrepreneur in his own right, put money into the original Ten business. He was clearly not put off by what happened because he invested at least one more time following the administration process. 'I have invested in getting on for 10 different companies, 3 or 4 of which have gone bust, and this is the only one that has done that,' he told me.

Another investor was Julie Meyer, founder of Ariadne Capital, an investment and advisory company that specializes in backing internet and media start-ups. She insisted to me that she still firmly believed Alex to be a man of integrity. She described Alex as a 'very fair, generous person', adding that he was the kind of founder that she wanted to succeed. Supporters like this are crucial if you find yourself in the kinds of problems Alex did. However, Julie also noted that keeping the investors happy was also a smart business move for someone who had found himself in such a difficult position and yet wanted to keep trading.

I have since spoken several times to Alex about his business. Ten has gone from strength to strength since it sought insolvency protection, an achievement that probably owes a lot to what Julie saw as Alex's focus on acting with integrity. When I asked Alex what he felt had been the greatest contribution to his entrepreneurial resurrection, he claimed it was due to building trust ahead of profits.

He added that there were moments of hope even in his darkest hour. In the dog days of 2003, he had a client who was willing to pay £2,000 for Wimbledon semi-final tickets. Ten managed to track some down for £1,000, but instead of charging as much as it could for them, added its standard 15 per cent margin. 'The question was, do we maximize our revenue or do we stand with our principles,' Alex said to me. 'I think that there is some karmic justice out there.'

Some believe that focusing on ethics rather than the bottom line is one of the reasons why companies such as Ten are forced into insolvency proceedings in the first place. Alex disagrees. 'I will be the most successful business in my market but that will be a by-product,' he said.

The example of Alex and his company is a challenge to the widespread perception, even among those who have gone into business themselves, that entrepreneurs only do it for the money.

However, as Alex found, this is not an easy path to follow. Perhaps the stigma of insolvency would be reduced if more entrepreneurs like Alex talked about their experiences of going through the process. Personally, I do not think that is going to happen any time soon, which is in many ways a shame.

Most societies still focus on eradicating business failure rather than encouraging those who get into problems to make good on what they have done. Focusing on the number of business failures also obscures the fact that many owner-managers have used economic turmoil and times of difficulty in their business to re-invent themselves and, perhaps, even make their ventures stronger as a result.

The conclusion

The point of all this is to say that failure is something every entrepreneur not only has to expect but should see as an opportunity to learn rather than give up.

The most important thing to do with failure is to act to resolve whatever has gone wrong in the most ethical way you can. As we have seen in this chapter, this may mean a difficult process, such as explaining your case to angry suppliers or unfortunate staff, but if you do not do this you will never be able to fully move on.

We have also seen that there are failings that are common and largely avoidable, such as maintaining healthy relations with the bank manager. These can be learnt and should be followed.

There is also no substitute for hard work, as well as no excuse for failure to learn from past mistakes.

According to the academics, the biggest threat to entrepreneurship is not failure but the fear of failure. If you do not start a business you may never fail, but you will also never be a successful entrepreneur.

Lastly, failure should be seen as an opportunity to improve. Only a small number of businesses survive, but even those will probably have tasted failure at least once. You never know, it may be the experience that turns you from an also-ran into a true rebel entrepreneur.

Index